Regulating for Trust in Journalism

Standards regulation in the age of blended media

Lara Fielden

REUTERS
INSTITUTE for the
STUDY of
JOURNALISM

UNIVERSITY OF
OXFORD

CITY UNIVERSITY
LONDON

Erratum:

p44 states that the Editors' Code of Practice is produced by the Society of Editors. It should state that the Editors' Code of Practice is written and reviewed by the Editors' Code of Practice Committee.

Contents

Summary of Text

1. **Introduction**
    1.1 2011 has been awash with investigations, consultations, scandals, and inquiries as Parliament, regulators, the courts and others respond to issues of journalistic standards
    1.2 Piecemeal responses fail to recognise and address the underlying conflict between converging media content and static standards regulation – broadcast, newspaper and video on demand content are increasingly indistinguishable, yet their regulation is disconnected and increasingly lacks the coherence and consistency on which public trust depends
    1.3 A new regulatory settlement is required: identifying the value and significance of media standards and enabling active participation by citizens in the public space across media platforms
    1.4 Chapter summary

2. **Background to the Regulation of Journalism in the UK**
    2.1 Statutory, licensed broadcasting regulation has developed in response to spectrum and information scarcity; self-regulation of the press has been accepted in the absence of regulatory leverage; video on demand services are 'co-regulated'; and other online content is largely unregulated
    2.2 The 2003 Communications Act established Ofcom as a 'converged' regulator for television, radio and telecoms but with no ambitions to regulate newspapers or the wider internet
    2.3 Debate over the next Communications Act has been initiated as an agenda for economic growth; this paper recommends an alternative democratic agenda that responds to convergence across the broadcast, newspaper, video on demand and wider online media platforms

3. **Television and Radio Regulation**
    3.1 A statutory regulator and code of comprehensive rules govern UK television and radio broadcast services, and assume that 'protection' of the public is both achievable and desirable
    3.2 Rules on due impartiality apply to broadcast services in relation to news and matters of public debate (case study: *The Great Global Warming Swindle*)
    3.3 A pragmatic approach is adopted towards international news services and impartiality rules may not be required (United States: the fairness doctrine)

3.4 The demands for impartiality originally linked to public service provision are applied across an extraordinary range of licensees, including news providers, often with radically different philosophies, global perspectives and associated audience expectations (case study: Press TV)

3.5 A diverse domestic community is also challenging 'generally accepted standards' (case study: Islam Channel)

3.6 The licensing of spectrum, and regulatory leverage it confers, is being challenged by digital switchover

3.7 The BBC has extended impartiality requirements, strengthening and widening consumer associations between impartiality and the BBC brand across media platforms (case study: 'How 1967 defined the Middle East')

4. Newspaper Regulation

4.1 A self-regulatory body and slim voluntary code applies to newspapers and magazines and is justified by the active selection and purchase of newspapers (by contrast to the traditional view of passive broadcasting consumption) and the freedom to publish in print (by contrast to the licensing of broadcasting)

4.2 Self-regulation of the press, challenged during successive periods of press impropriety has, in the absence of regulatory leverage, remained – but the current system has been significantly undermined

4.3 Self-regulation of newspapers has been justified against a backdrop of statutory regulation for television and radio, yet online newspapers are competing against the backdrop of the unregulated world of the internet (case study: the *Hamilton Advertiser*)

4.4 Proposal for independent regulation of the press: independent yet recognised in statute; voluntary yet robust in its requirements, expectations and sanctions; recognising the traditions of press freedom in print yet providing for the transparent regulation of online and other electronic press offerings (Ireland: independent, voluntary press regulation recognised in statute)

5. Video on Demand Regulation

5.1 Audiovisual content provided 'on demand' (whether via satellite, cable, mobile phone or internet) falls under a co-regulator, ATVOD, with backstop powers for Ofcom

5.2 Only two non-commercial, editorial rules apply to video on demand content, by contrast to the comprehensive Broadcasting Code (case study: *Frankie Boyle's Tramadol Nights;* and France: an interventionist approach)

5.3 A turf war has emerged between ATVOD and the PCC over newspapers providing video on demand content, and other providers are contesting ATVOD's authority (BNPtv: testing ATVOD's jurisdiction)

5.4 Current minimal regulation is out of line with audience expectations and with the value, and potential influence of video on demand content

5.5 The platform neutral approach of ATVOD (which is not linked to licensing and regulates on demand audiovisual content however it is received) may provide useful lessons for wider media regulation

6. Regulation of Wider Online Content

6.1 Online content is largely unregulated but may be subject to voluntary codes: YouTube, for example, 'crowdsources' regulation through its community guidelines

6.2 Bloggers have resisted suggestions of PCC regulation, relying instead on 'social capital' to demonstrate credibility (case study: *Spectator* blog)

6.3 A key driver towards more formal regulation of new media may be a desire for accreditation (Canada and Australia: defining the status of 'professional' journalists in a converged media landscape)

6.4 Public service duties extend to online content and should be matched by online standards requirements

7. The Consumer Perspective

7.1 Digital consumption demonstrates significant generational divides between the popularity of scheduled television and radio (favoured by older consumers) as compared to new media content (favoured by younger consumers)

7.2 Television is associated with familiarity and safety and consumers have expectations that video on demand services are subject to the same comprehensive regulation; the freedom and lack of boundaries associated with the internet are valued, and adult choices recognised, although protecting children and teenagers is a key concern

7.3 Television is a trusted source of news but the internet is more likely to be used as a source of news by younger than by older people; newspapers are declining as a source of local or international news

7.4 Impartiality on television and radio is generally considered important, but less so by younger people; the impartiality of television news is almost universally valued but impartiality for newspapers and the internet is also held to be important (when neither is required); audiences are sceptical about whether impartiality is achieved by broadcasters

7.5 Generational divides continue to underpin consumer preferences

8. Conclusions on Regulatory Challenges

8.1 Regulation is out of step with convergence

8.2 Regulation is out of step with public expectations, understanding, and requirements

8.3 Regulation is out of step with provider understanding, expectations, and requirements

8.4 Regulatory leverage is shifting

9. A Decade of Debate and Observations for the Next Decade

9.1 *New News Old News* (2002 ITC/BSC publication) made cautious recommendations to limit impartiality requirements to mainstream channels and for the regulation of public service content on the internet to be distinguished by 'kite marks'

9.2 James Murdoch's MacTaggart Lecture (2009) criticised regulation that treats the consumer as a passive creature in need of protection rather than as a customer who makes informed choices

9.3 Stewart Purvis's RTS Fleming Memorial Lecture (2010) called time on outdated regulation linked to analogue spectrum; he distinguished between 'public' and 'private' media and called for statutory powers to be focused where they were really needed

9.4 *Letting Children be Children* (2011) raised the issue of consistent protection for children across all media

List of Figures and Boxes

1. Introduction

1.1. 2011 – a year of media investigations, consultations, scandals, and inquiries

This is an extraordinary year in which to be writing about media regulation in the UK. In the first half of 2011 Culture Secretary Jeremy Hunt kick-started the debate on the next Communications Act with an open letter[1] setting out the Government's ambition, as part of its Plan for Growth, 'to establish UK communications and media markets as amongst the most dynamic and successful in the world'. He invited views on promoting growth, innovation, and deregulation. Shortly afterwards the Attorney-General announced that a Joint Committee drawn from both Houses of Parliament would be established[2] to consider 'the correct balance between privacy and freedom of expression', following the furore over the courts granting anonymity orders or 'super injunctions'. Then the Lord Chief Justice conducted a consultation[3] on whether twitter, email, and text messages could be permitted for fair and accurate court reporting by the media, and asked for help in defining who should be identified as 'the media': whether the term was limited to accredited, regulated journalists or also applied to unregulated bloggers and social commentators. The Government commissioned an Independent Review on the commercialisation and sexualisation of childhood from Mother's Union chair Reg Bailey, and in June 2011 the published report *Letting Children be Children*[4] concluded with recommendations for the media and its regulators. Next the House of Lords Select Committee on Communications produced its *Inquiry into the Governance and Regulation of the BBC*[5] and found itself baffled by the complexity of BBC complaints processes and concerned by the overlapping jurisdictions of the BBC Trust and Ofcom.

Then, in July, came the revelation that murdered school girl Milly Dowler's voicemail had been listened to, and on occasion deleted by, the *News of the World* and the full 'Hackgate' scandal exploded. The subsequent days saw the closure of *News of the World* and withdrawal of News Corporation's bid for BSkyB; resignations at the top of both the Metropolitan Police and News International; the Commons Culture, Media and Sport Committee hearings including the appearances of Rupert and James Murdoch; and the Prime Minister's announcement of a two-part inquiry under Lord Justice Leveson.[6] The inquiry was charged with 'making recommendations for a new, more effective way of

---

[1] http://www.culture.gov.uk/images/publications/commsreview-open-letter_160511.pdf.
[2] http://services.parliament.uk/hansard/Commons/bydate/20110523/mainchamberdebates/part003.html.
[3] http://www.judiciary.gov.uk/Resources/JCO/Documents/Consultations/cp-live-text-based-forms-of-comms.pdf.
[4] https://www.education.gov.uk/publications/eOrderingDownload/Bailey%20Review.pdf.
[5] http://www.publications.parliament.uk/pa/ld201012/ldselect/ldcomuni/166/16602.htm.
[6] http://www.publications.parliament.uk/pa/cm201011/cmhansrd/cm110713/debtext/110713-0001.htm.

regulating the press', and secondly with a full investigation into 'wrongdoing in the press and the police'.[7]

The golden thread of journalistic standards runs through each of these separate investigations, consultations, scandals, and inquiries; but pull the thread and the whole fabric of media regulation is in danger of unravelling. For while high-profile concerns about specific facets of regulation have surfaced with increasing regularity, underlying regulatory tensions have been developing that threaten long-term public confidence in journalism across the media landscape. Put most simply, converging media content is in conflict with static standards regulation, and unless the two are reconciled, public trust across media will be put at risk.

1.2. Conflict between converging media content and static standards regulation

As technologies advance apace, the media are characterised by mutation and convergence, while the standards regulating them are essentially static and divided. Newspapers are not just printed but online and carry video packages with the look and feel of traditional TV; broadcasters publish websites including text-based articles similar to online print offerings; scheduled programmes are broadcast but also available on-demand, on digital channels and a variety of websites; user-generated material vies for online audiences alongside professionally produced content; professional and amateur bloggers share the same debates.

Broadcast, newspaper, video on demand, and other online content are increasingly indistinguishable and yet regulated separately. Some material is subject to comprehensive rules set down by parliament, some to lighter touch statutory regulation, some to voluntary self-regulated rules, some to no regulatory authority at all. Accessed via a PC, smart phone, and tablet devices, regulated and unregulated content, licensed and unlicensed services, are becoming impossible to differentiate. Add to that the advent of internet-connected televisions and broadcast, video on demand, and online content will shortly sit side by side on the living room TV, further fuelling the potential for consumer confusion over whether the content with which they engage is regulated and, if so, to what extent and by whom.

This review argues that such regulatory incoherence risks undermining public trust across the broadcast, print, video on demand, and online media platforms, and public confidence in the sources of information on which citizens depend in order to make informed, democratic choices. Instead of supporting the public space[8] that exists across the media, conflicting regulation is increasingly undermining it.

Here evidence of confusion is identified over who regulates what, who deals with complaints, and where consumer expectations lie. Impartiality, for example, has been at the core of broadcasting requirements, partiality at the heart of newspaper freedom. As the two media converge this distinction begins to appear arbitrary and opaque. Meanwhile consumers' assumptions around video on demand are not met by the limited regulation that applies. Added to this, younger, converged consumers do not have the same reference points, such as brand associations, that to some extent assist older consumers in forming expectations around different content, and so differing regulation will appear increasingly illogical and ineffectual. At the same time services providing for diverse communities are increasingly challenging notions of generally accepted standards.

---

[7] The full terms of reference subsequently set out can be found at: http://www.levesoninquiry.org.uk/terms-of-reference-for-judge-led-inquiry.

[8] The term 'public space' is used in this paper to denote the sphere of democratic debate and engagement that exists across print, broadcast, video on demand, online, and other electronic media.

The most comprehensive regulation applies to broadcasting, and takes as its starting point the 'adequate protection' of the public. While protection of children is of considerable public concern, I ask whether 'protection' continues to be a meaningful ambition in relation to adult consumers, and consider the limitations on notions of protection when sources of content are unlimited and widely unregulated (given the context of the online content world). Is protection a desirable goal when, arguably, singling out broadcast content for comprehensive regulation gives a false sense of regulatory security, and leaves the consumer exposed and unprepared for the limited regulation of video on demand content, self-regulation of newspapers, and the unregulated global online world? This is particularly significant when the content derived from each may be indistinguishable.

There is evidence of an increasing sense of powerlessness amongst consumers and a regulatory framework that relies on 'dog whistles' rather than clarity and certainty in the navigation of journalistic content. Consideration of competing regulatory jurisdictions[9] reveals bewildering arrangements. Different regulators enforce different rules for a range of BBC material when broadcast on a BBC television channel; they differ again when that material is provided online, and again when provided by BBC Worldwide. The rules that apply to a commercial broadcaster's programming, when transmitted on a television channel, do not apply to their websites, and differ again when programmes are catalogued and provided as video on demand. Some newspapers accept the jurisdiction of a regulatory body, some do not; rules and regulators differ again for video content embedded into online newspaper articles, and again for newspapers that arrange video material in an online catalogue; they are different for blogs affiliated to the press, and differ again for those provided independently. And the distinctions between these rules are not trivial, they make the difference between impartial and partial content being permitted, between agreed obligations in relation to fair dealing and privacy or none, between accuracy being required for news or not, between a range of protections for children and young people or a minimal approach to harmful content.

One response to this extraordinary picture has been to demand a one-stop shop for consumer complaints. However, this fails to address the real cost of these opaque, inconsistent, and at times competing regimes. Without a coherent regulatory approach citizens cannot base their expectations of content on any consistent framework; they cannot sensibly evaluate its credibility nor make informed judgements about engagement with it; nor can they differentiate regulated and unregulated content in any meaningful way.

In addition to challenges for consumers, this review argues that regulation is out of step with the understanding, expectations, and requirements of providers. It identifies areas of duplication (between the BBC Trust and Ofcom), of tension (over the regulation of video on demand), and confusion (discussed above) which providers must negotiate, in addition to the recent discrediting of the Press Complaints Commission. It also argues that important opportunities are being missed, in the failure to support voluntary regulatory standards for currently unregulated, emerging content providers.

In addition, regulatory leverage is shifting. Democratic imperatives, but also pragmatic approaches, have always underpinned regulation, i.e. regulation is imposed where there is leverage over a provider. For broadcasting, the leverage provided by the allocation of analogue spectrum is receding and digital spectrum leverage is limited. Consideration of the purpose and practice of regulation across media platforms is required. Occupation of the regulated space will need to be incentivised, to ensure compliance in the future and to prevent migration to unregulated platforms provided online.

---

[9] Explored in Chs. 3–6 and illustrated in Annex 2.

Regulatory leverage is also shifting for print media. It is argued that the Press Complaints Commission's credibility has been undermined not just by the phone-hacking scandal, but by some newspaper titles operating with impunity outside its authority, and by the widening gap between the interests and ambitions of the broadsheet and red-top ends of the market.

Overall, it is contended here that current regulation, and the piecemeal attentions of recent inquiries and consultations, fails to address the democratic value in enabling the citizen to navigate and evaluate a range of journalism and other content – be it partial or impartial; regulated or unregulated; with public service commitments or purely commercial ambitions; and whether derived from broadcasting, print, video on demand or online.

1.3. A new regulatory settlement

The term 'standards' resonates in different ways through the shared public space provided across the media. Standards may seek to apply a restraining influence on content, in order to ensure that it reflects society's basic shared values, in keeping with audience expectations and measuring content against what is 'generally accepted'. Similarly it may seek to apply a restraining influence on journalistic and other content production practices, in order to curb excess and endeavour to ensure minimum standards of conduct, a sense of proportion and accountability. On the other hand standards may be aspirational, promoting content that encourages and enhances societal and cultural values. It may seek to inspire principled behaviour that represents a collective, professional set of values and recognition of the ethical, as well as legal, responsibilities that attach to influence.

Compulsory statutory regulation may be most easily associated with restraint, and voluntary self-regulation with aspiration, but here a flexible approach is proposed that allows these two qualities to meet in a new framework for media regulation. The proposed approach reflects statutory minimum requirements placed on some providers, while also incentivising transparent voluntary commitments to ethical standards, allowing the consumer to discriminate between the regulated and unregulated public space.

Recent responses to media standards have been defined by separate initiatives, discussed above, which lack connection and coherence. Instead, I argue that a new overarching settlement for media regulation is required in which parliament, regulators, providers, and consumers would each play their part. In launching the initial consultation on a new Communications Bill, referred to above, the stated intention of the Culture Secretary was to frame the debate, or at least its first stage, in terms of economic growth. I do not dispute the importance of the communications sector to the growth of the UK economy,[10] but the aim here is to carve out a democratic rather than economic agenda in the key area of standards regulation.

Under the approach proposed, a new regulatory settlement for both consumers and providers would be established.

---

[10] *Creative UK: The Audiovisual Sector and Economic Success,* by Robin Foster and Tom Broughton, estimates that 'around £13bn of funds flowing through the audiovisual economy, supporting direct production to the value of over £4bn, and as many as 132,000 direct UK jobs': www.commcham.com/publications/creative-uk.

- Consumers would be enabled to access, navigate, and engage with journalism, and wider media content, as active, informed citizens who make choices about media content. A transparent regulatory framework would support them in differentiating regulated from unregulated journalism and other content; in basing their expectations of a range of regulated content on clear, straightforward signposting across platforms; and in making choices accordingly. In addition, appropriate protections would be provided for the vulnerable, including, most importantly, children.
- Providers would also be invited to make choices, in keeping with their values and business models. The current comprehensive statutory requirements for all broadcasting would be narrowed to public service content, and applied across media platforms. In addition, baseline requirements for television and video on demand content, agreed at a European level, would be acknowledged and applied. Between the upper and lower ends of this targeted statutory framework however, providers would be incentivised to subscribe to a new model of independent, voluntary regulation (discussed below).

This would represent a new compact including citizens, journalists and other media providers, regulators, and Parliament in its development. It would recognise that, in order to provide a proportionate and consistent approach to regulation across the media, some current regulatory expectations would be reduced (with a deregulatory approach to non-public service broadcast content) and others developed (incentivising consistent independent regulation of journalism and other content across online and video on demand, newspaper, and commercial broadcast services). This realigning of provider duties and consumer expectations will undoubtedly present challenges, however its ambition, as discussed in Chapter 10, is to provide coherence and clarity. It proposes a redistribution and evening of requirements across a media landscape whose regulation is increasingly characterised, as demonstrated here, by inconsistency and confusion.

The proposal is not for an overnight transformation of the regulatory landscape for the media, but rather for managed transition: enabling consumers, providers, and regulators to recognise historic expectations of media delivery, but play catch-up with technological advances and content convergence, equipping them with a flexible regulatory framework ready to adapt to future transformations of the electronic media landscape. Transitional arrangements under a new Communications Act would move the regulation of journalism, and wider content provision within which it sits, towards a new cross-media tiered regulatory framework that provides for the range of content across the public space based on core characteristics explored in Chapter 10 and summarised here.

A regulatory framework that enables citizens and protects children
This review argues that the current Communications Act blurs protections that are necessary for children with an approach that unhelpfully casts adults as passive consumers on whom content is imposed. It argues for an approach that properly protects the vulnerable while enabling citizens to make informed, active choices about engaging (or not engaging) with content across media platforms.

Under this approach, requirements within the next Communications Act would differentiate between providers in whom there is a public interest, through, for example, public ownership, funding, and/or subject to public service obligations, and those that represent purely private interests, commercial or otherwise. Instead of regulation attaching to the method of delivery (broadcast, newspapers, video on demand) as is currently the case, it would be determined by the nature of the content, and the values of its provider, across media platforms. Three tiers of standards regulation, each denoted by an associated standards mark, would target requirements and thereby enable citizens and consumers to access a varied, but coherent, public space across broadcast, print, video on demand, and related online services.

Comprehensive 'premium standard' regulation of public service providers across media platforms (Tier 1)

The proposed regulatory settlement would provide a clear, statutory, understanding of the value of, and expectations around, 'public' content providers with public service duties and privileges. It would set out 'premium standard' statutory requirements for media providing public service content (the BBC, Channel 4, S4C, and currently ITV[11] and Channel 5) across all media platforms including related websites and video on demand provision.

These 'public' providers would be expected to play a role in supporting consumers in navigating online content and to counter concerns that fragmented new media serve to reinforce prejudices and narrow horizons. Comprehensive rules, potentially not dissimilar to the current Ofcom Code but based on a principle of enabling citizens and protecting children, would apply. Impartiality requirements would provide access to balanced coverage and a range of viewpoints on issues of particular public significance and debate. Under the approach proposed, commercial public service providers would be incentivised to continue to maintain their commitment to public service provision through such benefits as EPG prominence and enhanced access to audiences via the public service multiplexes.[12] Standards requirements would be part of the expectations placed on them, but also a transparent demonstration of excellence and authority, associating them with media organisations under public ownership, and differentiating their offerings from the rest of the industry.

The rules would be set out in statute and administered and enforced by a regulator with statutory powers, the level of requirements would be clearly identified by a 'Tier 1' standards mark on electronic programme guides (EPGs) and online.

Initially this top tier of regulation could apply across broadcasting. However, a new Communications Act would open up the possibility of other providers, perhaps whose selling point is their impartiality, affiliating themselves with this tier. Over time this could include video on demand services, newspapers, and any other online providers. Similarly, over time private broadcasters (without public service obligations) could elect to move to either of the two following tiers of regulation.

Independent regulation of private (non-public service) providers across platforms (Tier 2)

It is proposed that a new model of 'independent' regulation should be introduced, initially for the press and, as it develops, open to non-public service media across platforms.

The history of press regulation, and periodic surfacing of debates on statutory requirements, is discussed in Chapter 4. The historic tension between 'licensing' the press

---

[11] Including STV, UTV, and Channel Television.

[12] By the completion of digital switch over in 2012, it is predicted that services carried on the public service multiplexes will be available to 98.5% of the population while the commercial multiplexes' transmission network will cover around 90% of the population. This is because 'The commercial multiplexes ... have concluded that they cannot justify the very substantial investment in additional DTT transmission capacity to reach the final 10 per cent of the UK population': http://stakeholders.ofcom.org.uk/binaries/research/tv-research/no3factsheet.pdf.

and rights to freedom of speech are examined; the balance between rights and responsibilities, between press freedom and accountability, is revealed to be a delicate one.

Here a regulatory model is offered in which the press would retain the freedoms and privileges on which its journalism is founded but would also have a voluntary but clear mechanism for acknowledging the duties and responsibilities that accompany them. It would be incentivised to adhere to robustly enforced standards, as a demonstration of those commitments in print and online, and consumers would be provided with clarity over whether individual titles choose to operate within the regulated or unregulated public space. Under this approach the following key principles would govern press regulation in addition to the wider transparency requirement discussed below:

Independence – This second tier of regulation would be independent of both state and industry, recognised by both but beholden to neither. It would be funded, and its rules established, by industry, but the independence of its decision-making and robustness of its sanctions would be assured.

Statutory recognition – The proposed model of regulation would be provided with recognition in statute. This would lay a secure foundation for its authority and independence, including the composition and independence of its board and adjudicating panels, and a recognition of a range of procedures and sanctions. It would not confer statutory powers, since the basis for its authority would be voluntary membership, but would provide a link to a number of significant privileges associated with membership (discussed below).

Incentivised voluntary participation – Newspapers, in print and online, and wider journalists and bloggers, would have the choice of electing standards as a selling point through this model of regulation and enjoying associated benefits. Conversely they could choose to operate outside the regulated sphere and simply within the law, as is the case for unregulated online content. Benefits and privileges could include accreditation in relation to court reporting and other privileged access to information, attractive advertising associations, recognition of affiliation by the courts in any privacy or libel proceedings. Those newspapers operating outside the regulated sphere would be understood by the public to have rejected such an association and would be unable to demonstrate their ethical standards through this framework and associated standards mark.

Credible investigations and sanctions – In return for the benefits of membership, the regulated press would be required to agree and accept a range of sanctions and investigatory procedures at the disposal of the new regulatory body, including suspension and expulsion from its membership and associated benefits.

Transition – Over time the proposal would be to extend the model of Tier 2 independent regulation to 'private' media across all platforms, on a voluntary basis. In this way private media would be incentivised to elect to adhere to voluntary ethical standards drawn up by the media industry. The standards could be nuanced for the provision of content across broadcast, print, video on demand, and online platforms and apply to any provider seeking to differentiate their offering by adherence to them.

Consistency with the baseline regulation for broadcast and video on demand services agreed at a European level (Tier 3)

For providers deciding not to make the commitment to standards set out in Tier 2, statutory requirements would be set out as a baseline of regulation for all 'private' broadcast and video on demand providers consistent with the demands of European agreed standards. Requirements could include protection of the under-18s, a prohibition on incitement to hatred, and commercial obligations. These requirements would be compulsory only for broadcast and video on demand services (including any provided by newspapers). However, over time it could be open to newspapers (in print and online) to level down from Tier 2 to Tier 3 (sacrificing associated benefits and privileges), meanwhile currently unregulated online providers could elect to opt in to this level of regulation as a mark of basic standards.

Transparency

Each regulatory tier would be required to be signalled by a transparent 'standards mark' displayed on electronic programme guides (EPGs) and in print; similarly the relevant standards mark would be clearly flagged on websites or other electronic media. The standards mark would provide not just mainstream providers but, significantly, new brands, with transparent messaging for the public. It would readily identify providers subscribing to each tier, and also attach to individual content provided via online content aggregators.

An inclusive framework for new media providers

The ambition of the proposed settlement would be both to manage transition by establishing a framework that first introduces consistency of regulation for those providers currently subject to statutory or self-regulation, but secondly provides sufficient flexibility so that the framework can be developed and offered to emerging providers (on a voluntary basis) over time.

It would be open to any media provider not caught by the compulsory regulation of Tiers 1 and 3 to 'opt in' to any of the three tiers of regulation. A blogger could, for example, seek accreditation through voluntary affiliation with a chosen tier. Similarly a commercial provider subject only to minimal requirements could elect to join a tier offering enhanced regulation if that were considered advantageous to their offering. Going forward, newspapers, as their online content becomes an increasingly significant part of their offering, could seek association with any of the three tiers. Broadsheets and tabloids could, for example, elect regulation under different tiers depending on which most closely reflected their values and content. The proposed framework is not limited to audiovisual material, but would be offered to any electronic media provider as the media landscape develops.

1.4. Chapter summary

This report is specifically concerned with the regulation of UK journalism, within a context of wider content regulation, though it considers a variety of international examples of developing regulation and responses to converging content. It also explores the context of European Union legislation within which UK regulation must operate. It draws on a series of interviews conducted in May 2011. Interviewees, from a range of regulatory, broadcast, print, and academic backgrounds, were invited to reflect on the interconnected nature of the media and its future regulation. My analysis and recommendations have benefited from their insightful responses to the challenge of media convergence. While the interviews do not reflect on the subsequent repercussions of the phone-hacking revelations, they provide thoughtful, informed contributions on the underlying challenges facing UK standards regulation as well as international perspectives.

In the first part, Chapters 2 to 6 explore the regulatory requirements placed on broadcasting, print media, video on demand content, and wider online regulation. These chapters consider how these differing requirements have emerged, and how they are challenged by the convergence of media content. In particular they examine requirements for, and expectations of, impartiality. They explore where regulatory requirements are beginning to buckle under the strain of an increasingly blended media environment, in which spectrum scarcity and information scarcity are no longer the prime movers in determining the regulatory framework.

These chapters are informed by the observations of interviewees, illustrated by a range of case studies and supported by relevant consumer research set out in Chapter 7. Chapter 8 concludes with observations on current regulatory inconsistencies and uncertainties, arguing that content regulation has fallen out of step with the pace of convergence and with the understanding, expectations, and requirements of both the public and of content providers. As Richard Sambrook put it: 'technology is running ahead of our ability to manage it'.[13]

> We are moving from a world where you've had limited provision – and therefore greater responsibilities that could be placed upon those limited providers through regulation – to a world of enormous supply and choice where regulation really is going to be very difficult to enforce. And therefore we are moving from a world where the consumer can be protected through regulation to a world where they are going to have to be far better educated in understanding what they consume and how they consume it. And the difficulty at the minute is that we are caught in the kind of rapids in the middle.

The final part seeks a way out of the 'rapids' in which we find ourselves. Chapter 9 considers key reports and lectures from the last decade that have contributed to our understanding of the challenges posed by media converging on the same space. It then outlines ideas and perspectives contributed by those interviewed. It includes lessons from international ambitions for a unified 'cross-media' code, and consideration of the importance of cultural expectations, consumer awareness, and of voluntary aspirations for ethical standards in journalism.

Chapter 10 argues that we must negotiate a period of managed transition as we move on from the familiar protections of television and radio and navigate the blurred world of regulated and unregulated content. It seeks to consider how the underlying democratic function of journalistic content can best be enhanced, and the public and providers best served, in a new approach to its regulation. It outlines a tiered and targeted framework, which is transparently messaged for the consumer across media platforms, and provides a combination of statutory and independent, voluntary requirements both for existing and new providers. It takes as its starting point the objective of *enabling*, rather than *protecting*, the public and, in addition, incentivises providers to see regulation as a selling point – a way of differentiating their offering in an increasingly competitive, global market – rather than as a burdensome constraint.

---

[13] Interview May 2011.

The next Communications Act and, more immediately, the inquiries set up in recent months to consider aspects of journalistic values and practice, face the difficulty and opportunity of distilling what we value about the public space and regulating it, consistently and proportionately, across platforms. The aim here is to carve out, at the heart of debate on the future communications framework, this democratic agenda.

2. Background to the Regulation of Journalism in the UK

2.1. A range of regulatory regimes for increasingly indistinguishable content

The creatures outside looked from pig to man, and from man to pig, and from pig to man again; but already it was impossible to say which was which.

As consumers look from television content streamed live over the internet, to audiovisual content provided by online newspapers; as they select BBC clips from YouTube, alongside user-generated home videos; as they anticipate the imminent arrival of internet-connected televisions where heavily regulated, scheduled 'linear' content will sit side by side with lightly regulated, self-scheduled video on demand content, and alongside global content of indeterminate regulatory requirements, they could be forgiven for feeling as much confusion as the creatures in George Orwell's *Animal Farm*. As technologies converge, even our reference points begin to break down. Can 'broadcasting', an already elastic term encompassing not just broadcast provision but also cable and satellite, be used to describe the provision of content over the internet? Can 'television' meaningfully describe services when divorced from the box in the living room and provided online? If 'newspapers' are online what is their connection with 'paper' and 'print'? And beyond confusions over audiovisual content and its terminology are the questions of how – and more significantly, why – we regulate content standards, not just for adults, but also for the children and young people consuming, providing, and engaging with it.

The focus here is on the how and why of standards regulation: across broadcast, newspapers, video on demand, and wider online content, whether provided on the 'four screens' of televisions, laptops, smart phones, and tablets or in print.

Broadcasting standards regulation in the UK has developed in response to the demands of scarcity, specifically spectrum scarcity and information scarcity. Access to limited spectrum, and through spectrum to audiences, has been the reward in return for which broadcasters, from the smallest local radio stations to national players, have hitherto accepted comprehensive regulation that would be considered entirely unacceptable in other areas of the media. It is on the basis of this regulatory leverage over spectrum that the system of broadcast licences and rules on standards in broadcasting have been built and employed for social and cultural purposes.

Meanwhile, information scarcity has traditionally underpinned the key demands placed on broadcast journalism, and most particularly the requirements for impartiality. These requirements have sought to promote access to trustworthy information on which the public can base informed decisions as democratic citizens. At the same time they check the potential for the medium to manipulate public opinion, and for the State and others to exert a harmful influence over both broadcasting and its audiences.[14] Television and radio, traditionally cast as 'guests in the living room', pushing content out to audiences, have attracted a range of further safeguards designed to protect the viewing and listening public, and in particular children, from harm and offence. In addition, requirements are set out to protect members of the public involved in, or the subjects of, programmes from unfair treatment and unwarranted infringement of their privacy (reflecting the requirements of the European Audiovisual Media Services Directive and the European Convention on Human Rights respectively).

Print journalism, however, does not attract the same protections and this has been justified through a different narrative. Buying a newspaper is seen as a more active expression of choice, and one which does not expose the purchaser to the same degree of influence as the broadcast media. Indeed, the partisan approach of the press is celebrated as an active demonstration of freedom of expression. While statutory regulation over the press has been periodically discussed, usually at times of tabloid impropriety, successive parliamentary Select Committees have demonstrated a pragmatic acceptance of self-regulation. In the absence of any regulatory leverage (equivalent to the system of licences that has underpinned the broadcasting model) the self-regulatory consensus has continued, although at the time of writing this is subject to scrutiny by the Leveson Inquiry.

European requirements have resulted in a new form of regulation for video on demand or 'VOD' services under the Authority for Television On Demand (ATVOD). Previously the 'Association' for Television On Demand, ATVOD was set up following the Communications Act of 2003 as a self-regulatory industry body for emerging video on demand services (typically providing seven-day catch-up services for material previously broadcast). From 2010 ATVOD took on the mantle of Ofcom's co-regulator. It requires providers of video on demand services, offering programmes comparable to those shown on traditional television channels, to notify ATVOD of their existence, pay the required fee, and abide by the regulation demanded under the EU Audiovisual Media Services (AVMS) Directive. This regulation is minimal by comparison to rules for broadcasting and its light touch approach is justified by the argument that video on demand material is 'pulled' by audiences rather than 'pushed' on to them, although it will be argued here that this distinction is rapidly losing relevance. Video on demand services, whether provided by means of the internet, cable, satellite, or digital terrestrial television, whether received on a television set, laptop, or smart phone, all fall within ATVOD's regulation.

Finally, we have witnessed the rapid explosion of the internet. Its multiple purposes, lack of any central organisation, and its global reach explain the obvious difficulties in imposing any meaningful regulation over it and challenge assumptions of national jurisdiction. And, in any event, even the limited regulation imposed on video on demand internet-based services has been fiercely resisted by those who argue that it runs counter to everything that is valued about the internet's creative, if anarchic, energy. With the internet providing access to information on a scale previously unimaginable, fears over the monopoly of information may decline, but concerns over distinguishing the quality and trustworthiness of that information heighten. At the same time there is concern over

---

[14] Explored by Tim Suter, *The Price of Plurality* (2008): http://reutersinstitute.politics.ox.ac.uk/uploads/media/The_Price_of_Plurality_01.pdf.

Delivery	Regulation	Requirements	Scope	Regulator
Broadcasting	Statutory regulation	Comprehensive statutory standards requirements protecting the under-eighteens, on harm and offence, crime, religion, due impartiality and due accuracy, elections and referendums, fairness, privacy and commercial communications.	• Applies to all content on UK television and radio broadcasts (but not, for example, to associated websites which may include audio and audiovisual material, or YouTube offerings) from the same brand. • BBC accuracy, impartiality and certain commercial requirements are regulated by the BBC Trust. • Not open to non-broadcast providers seeking regulation.	**Ofcom** Administration and enforcement underpinned by statutory powers. Plus, in the case of the BBC, certain standards responsibilities for the **BBC Trust**
Newspapers	Self regulation	Voluntary clauses, drawn up by industry, on accuracy, opportunity to reply, privacy, intrusion into grief or shock, children, hospitals, reporting of crime, clandestine devices and subterfuge, victims of sexual assault, discrimination, financial journalism, confidential sources, payments to witnesses and criminals.	• Applies to UK newspapers and magazines that accept the PCC's jurisdiction, in print and/or online (which may include audio and audiovisual material and blogs). • For VOD material see below. • Open to independent bloggers to sign up to PCC membership. Remit being extended to members' tweets.	**Press Complaints Commission (PCC)** Administration and enforcement underpinned by voluntary membership (some newspaper titles do not accept the jurisdiction of the PCC and are unregulated).
Video On Demand (VOD)	Co-regulation	Statutory rules on incitement to hatred and material that might seriously impair under-18s; plus commercial rules on sponsorship and product placement.	• Applies to the editorial content of VOD programme services (however they are distributed). • A number of newspaper, broadcaster and other providers dispute ATVOD's authority over their content.	**ATVOD** Administration and enforcement underpinned by partnership with industry but with backstop powers for Ofcom. BBC VOD content falls under BBC Trust or Ofcom or ATVOD depending on BBC or non BBC delivery.
Other online/ electronic content	Elements of self-regulation Civil and criminal law applies	Self-regulation, for example, to minimise the availability of criminal content (e.g. child sexual abuse images) or offensive content (e.g. user-generated material on YouTube).	• Providers choosing to adopt self-regulation.	Regulation in limited areas. Examples: Internet Watch Foundation (IWF) YouTube Community Guidelines Note: BBC and other individual broadcasters are responsible for their websites including audiovisual material on them (unless deemed 'VOD'); and for online content via RadioPlayer.

Figure 2.1: Summary of current delivery-based standards regulation

the ease with which the internet can filter consumers' sources of information and narrow their horizons to consumption of material that amounts to nothing more than what has been dubbed 'The Daily Me'.[15]

Figure 2.1 briefly summarises the current distinctions between media regulation which are explored in more detail in Chapters 3 to 6 below. In addition, Annex 2 illustrates the complexities of related consumer complaint handling.

Looked at from the perspective of the historic development, and differing purposes, of diverse content platforms and modes of publication, there is a logic to this range and partitioning of regulation. However, when looked at from the perspective of increasingly indistinguishable content, rather than the platform on which it is published, this logic rapidly falls away.

2.2. Ofcom – a 'converged' regulator

When Ofcom was established in 2003 it took over the duties of five regulators whose responsibilities were previously distinct. Oftel licensed and regulated telecoms services, the Radiocommunications Agency licensed and regulated radio spectrum, the Independent Television Commission ('ITC') licensed and regulated commercial television, the Radio Authority licensed and regulated commercial radio, and the Broadcasting Standards Commission ('BSC') was responsible for matters relating to taste, decency, fairness, and privacy in relation to all broadcasters including the BBC. Ofcom was heralded as the 'converged' regulator.

Lord Currie, Ofcom's first Chairman, defined Ofcom's embodiment of convergence in three ways: first, its 'duties across broadcasting, telecommunications and spectrum'; secondly, its ability to 'balance the demands of economic regulation, competition, consumers and markets, with the demands of content and cultural regulation, public service and public interest, the citizen'; and thirdly, that it was 'not organised within silos dealing with television, radio, telecoms'.[16] With the advent of Ofcom some of the duplications in regulation that had previously existed were swept away. For example, complaints about standards on commercial television had previously been considered by both the ITC (which investigated whether a licensee had breached its licence in any broadcast) and the BSC (responsible for adjudicating on complaints about standards and fairness) until Ofcom took over the duties of both bodies.[17]

The Communications Act 2003 that established Ofcom was radical in demolishing the organisational and legislative barriers, and overlapping responsibilities, between television, radio, and telecoms. It had no ambitions, however, with regard to either newspapers or the wider internet, although in relation to the latter Currie recognised the future 'awkward choices' that would have to be made when he addressed the European Competitive Telecommunication Association in December 2003:

> *When the Internet can deliver what looks to all intents and purposes like television broadcasting in a few years' time, then Ofcom and the Government will face awkward choices. Should, in the interests of fairness, the content regulation of terrestrial, cable and satellite broadcasting be rolled out to*

---

[15] H. Margetts, *The Price of Plurality* (2008): http://reutersinstitute.politics.ox.ac.uk/uploads/media/The_Price_of_Plurality_01.pdf.

[16] D. Currie, 'The Principles and Objectives of a Converged Communications Regulator', 4th ECTA Regulatory Conference, 10 Dec. 2003: http://media.ofcom.org.uk/2003/12/10/4th-ecta-regulatory-conference-10-december-2003.

[17] As discussed in Ch. 3, duplications still exist between the BBC Trust and Ofcom; complainants can request either body to investigate and adjudicate (except in relation to impartiality and accuracy where only the BBC Trust is responsible).

Internet broadcasters? Or should the content regulation of terrestrial, cable and satellite broadcasters be significantly rolled back, passing the baton to smart navigational devices that allow people to find the content that they want (subject to the law) and avoid the content that they do not want to see or hear?

It is these 'awkward choices' that now require urgent attention, arising as they do from the continuing and rapid development of convergence across broadcast and online content.

If a single screen can provide the consumer with a blend of content from a mainstream broadcaster, an online newspaper, a video on demand service, and an internet blogger, all at the same time, perhaps even all authored by the same journalist, then the wholly different regulatory regimes to which each element is subject begin to feel increasingly arbitrary and irrational both to consumers and providers. Nor, whether consumed separately or in combination, is the regulation transparent, and therefore meaningful, to the public. It fails to enable the public to discriminate between regulated and unregulated content, and to make informed choices and selections. Instead brand associations may be relied on which, as we shall see, can be misleading and in particular fail to support younger consumers and newer providers.

2.3. An economic or democratic agenda for media regulation?

With preparations for a new Communications Bill underway, and a Green Paper due to be published before the end of 2011, a reappraisal of the traditional regulatory architecture in relation to content standards has already begun. Mark Thompson, at a Whitehall seminar on impartiality in broadcasting in December 2010, was reported as saying:

There was a logic in allowing impartial broadcasters to have a monopoly of the broadcasting space. But in the future, maybe there should be a broad range of choices. Why shouldn't the public be able to see and hear, as well as read, a range of opinionated journalism and then make up their own mind what they think about it?[18]

Culture Secretary Jeremy Hunt told the Oxford Media Convention in January 2011: 'I pose the question as to the way we regulate the internet compared to the way we regulate traditional broadcasting. Today they are completely different and maybe we have to accept that difference. But maybe we can bridge that gap.'[19] He declared:

I am prepared to radically rethink the way we do things. To take a fresh look at what we regulate, whether we regulate and how we regulate. To consider whether there are areas we might move out of regulation altogether. And to think hard about what we mean by public service content. As parents we want programmes to be suitable for our children. As citizens we want impartial news. And as consumers we want high-quality programmes we know and trust. Whether we're watching a broadcast live or though catch-up services, via a TV or a computer, it's the content that matters, rather than the delivery mechanism. So should it continue to be the case that the method of delivery has a significant impact on the method of regulation? Or should

---

[18] *Guardian*, 17 Dec. 2010.
[19] http://www.guardian.co.uk/media/2011/jan/19/jeremy-hunt-online-tv.

we be looking at a more platform-neutral approach? What do we need to do to help our businesses grow and evolve between now and 2025? Where can regulation help and where is it a barrier? What can we do collectively to enhance the whole UK market? This is not about tweaking the current system, but redesigning it – from scratch if necessary – to make it fit for purpose.[20]

On 16 May 2011 he opened debate on 'A Communications Review for the Digital Age' with an open letter,[21] and a YouTube invitation for views on a number of questions concerning growth, innovation, and deregulation, explaining:

Our ambition is to establish UK communications and media markets as amongst the most dynamic and successful in the world, with the review process culminating in a new communications framework by 2015, to support the sector for the next 10 years and beyond.

The letter explained that this significant agenda was at the heart of the Government's wider policy set out in Plan for Growth[22] and that 'The aim is to put the UK on the path to sustainable, long-term economic growth'.

While the interests of citizens and consumers were referred to in the open letter, its stated intention was to frame the debate, or at least this initial stage, in terms of economic growth. The aim here, however, is to establish, at the heart of debate on the future communications framework, a democratic rather than economic agenda. In the key area of standards regulation, the new framework, at its core, should serve to enable active participation in the public space that exists across platforms, through informed choice. Also, the requirement to 'protect citizens' referred to in the open letter should be challenged. How far is this goal is achievable, or even desirable, and should the protection of children rather than adults be prioritised?

Rather than a wholesale 'rolling out' of regulation to the internet or the wholesale 'rolling back' of current broadcast regulation, touched upon in Lord Currie's remarks (above), this work seeks to explore a more nuanced 'redistributive' approach to standards regulation across platforms. I begin by reflecting on the very different regulatory requirements outlined above. What do these reveal about the democratic value currently placed on journalism, across broadcast, print and internet content; what is understood by the responsibilities attached to journalism; and how far do we currently regulate because we 'can' rather than because we 'should'?

The justification for the varied approach to regulation across the different media is woven into the narrative that accompanies each area (the familiar depictions of 'guests in the living room', 'active choices', and 'anarchic energy' briefly rehearsed above in relation to broadcasting, print, and the internet respectively). However, it is my contention that these narratives are in fact bolted on to a very pragmatic approach: where we can regulate we do; where we cannot, because we lack the 'big stick' of regulatory leverage, we tell a different story about democratic imperatives and public protections, adopt a realistic position, and apply different (or no) regulatory requirements.

The following review of the current regulation of journalism provides an overview of how, and why, the widely different regulatory frameworks for television, radio, print, video on demand content, and the internet, together with the array of statutory, co-, and self-regulatory bodies, have arisen within the context of both UK and related European

---

[20] http://image.guardian.co.uk/sys-files/Media/documents/2011/01/24/OMC-Hunt.pdf.
[21] http://www.culture.gov.uk/images/publications/commsreview-open-letter_160511.pdf.
[22] http://cdn.hm-treasury.gov.uk/2011budget_growth.pdf.

legislation. It does not seek to separate the regulation of journalism from the context of wider media regulation in which it sits, but rather to provide a broad understanding of different, and at times competing, at times inconsistent, regulatory structures currently in place. It attempts to distil their overall democratic function and value, and what they reveal about the democratic value placed on journalism and wider content across different contexts.

Exploring, for example, the requirements around impartiality and freedom of speech, it uses a range of case studies to illustrate the practical application of statutory broadcasting regulation, and compares this with the self-regulation of print and online newspapers, and the very limited internet regulation, for example, in relation to video on demand content. The case studies include published adjudications (from Ofcom, the Trust, the PCC, and ATVOD) highlighting material found to have breached, and not to have breached, the current regulations, and, sometimes most interestingly, material on the cusp.

3. Television and Radio Regulation

Regulatory scrutiny and enforcement are applied to content broadcast on all UK television and radio services. Richard Hooper, Ofcom's first Content Board Chairman, introducing the first Broadcasting Code in 2005 published by the new regulator Ofcom, addressed the democratic value of broadcasting when he described the 'critical power' of broadcast media 'to shape our opinions as citizens and to inform democratic debate' and continued:

> *Freedom of expression is at the heart of any democratic state. It is an essential right to hold opinions and receive and impart information and ideas. Broadcasting and freedom of expression are intrinsically linked. However, with such rights come duties and responsibilities.*

He celebrated a delicate regulatory balancing act between rights and duties enshrined in the new Broadcasting Code:

> *The setting out of clear principles and rules [in the Broadcasting Code] will allow broadcasters more freedom for creativity and audiences greater freedom to exercise their choices, while securing those objectives set by Parliament.*[23]

James Murdoch, guest speaker at an Ofcom conference the following year, took a very different view of the Broadcasting Code and argued that broadcasting regulation in the UK crippled the sector:

> *We often think of broadcasting as a special case. The dead hand of history is to blame ... From the very start UK broadcasting regulation was skewed. Not to protect people against real harm, but to ensure that broadcasting was a sort of moral and educative crusade.*[24]

So how tightly is the broadcasting sector regulated, is there a place for a 'moral and educative' purpose, and how dead, or otherwise, is the hand of history?

[23] http://stakeholders.ofcom.org.uk/binaries/broadcast/Broadcast-Code-2005.pdf.
[24] Ofcom conference, Nov. 2006: http://www.guardian.co.uk/media/2006/nov/30/citynews.television.

3.1. A statutory regulator 'protects' the public

Ofcom has a statutory duty to apply the Broadcasting Code to its over 2,000 licensed services, which in turn are required to observe the Broadcasting Code under the terms of their licences.[25] The Broadcasting Code sets out 173 comprehensive rules,[26] and practices to be followed, covering the protection of under-18s, harm, offence, crime, religion, due impartiality, due accuracy, undue prominence of views and opinions, elections and referendums, fairness, privacy, and commercial matters. The Broadcasting Code includes rules on issues as diverse as 'exorcism, the occult and the paranormal', 'drugs, smoking, solvents and alcohol', and 'surreptitious filming or recording' and is periodically updated. In 2009 rules on sexual material, competitions, and voting were strengthened following high-profile breaches. Following the Government's decision to permit product placement in certain genres of programmes, the rules on commercial messaging in radio and television were relaxed in 2010 and 2011 respectively. The rules, supplemented by notes and meanings, provide the framework within which all broadcast content, including, therefore, broadcast journalism, must operate.

Detailed additional guidance notes accompany each section of rules, and breaches of the Code can result in sanctions ranging from a published finding through to significant financial and other penalties including licence revocation. The Broadcasting Code applies only to broadcast material and while broadcasters can, and do, contact Ofcom for advice prior to broadcast, the regulator's remit is to investigate potential breaches of the Code after transmission, not to act as a 'censor' beforehand.

The statutory basis for the Broadcasting Code, derived from the Communications Act (2003), differentiates it from the self-regulation of the press, and informs the detail and articulation of the rules. Specifically section 3(2) of the Act charges Ofcom with securing broadcasting standards that provide 'adequate protection' to members of the public from 'offensive and harmful material', 'unfair treatment', and 'unwarranted infringements of privacy'. The Act sets out specific 'standards objectives' which include protection of under-18s and a prohibition on material likely to encourage or incite crime or disorder.

Broadcasting regulation is constrained by the articles of the EU Audiovisual Media Services (AVMS) Directive[27] and any future regulatory settlement for the UK will have to give effect to its provisions. Agreed at a European level, the Directive sets out certain minimum requirements for television broadcasting which are reflected in the Broadcasting Code. These include commercial provisions designed to create a level playing field for member states in relation to sponsorship, advertising, and product placement and other commercial communications, including prohibitions around news. The Directive also contains the prohibition of any incitement to hatred based on race, sex, religion, or nationality; rules to protect minors from material such as pornography and extreme violence; and requirements for a right of reply where 'legitimate interests, in particular reputation and good name, have been damaged by an assertion of incorrect facts'.

---

[25] Certain sections of the Broadcasting Code do not apply to the BBC and are discussed further below.
[26] http://stakeholders.ofcom.org.uk/broadcasting/broadcast-codes/broadcast-code.
[27] http://eur-lex.europa.eu/LexUriServ/LexUriServ.do?uri=OJ:L:2010:095:0001:0024:EN:PDF.

Box 1. Extracts from the EU Audiovisual Media Services Directive applicable to television broadcasting (non-commercial editorial provisions)

Article 6
Member States shall ensure by appropriate means that audiovisual media services provided by media service providers under their jurisdiction do not contain any incitement to hatred based on race, sex, religion or nationality.

Article 27
1. Member States shall take appropriate measures to ensure that television broadcasts by broadcasters under their jurisdiction do not include any programmes which might seriously impair the physical, mental or moral development of minors, in particular programmes that involve pornography or gratuitous violence.

2. The measures provided for in paragraph 1 shall also extend to other programmes which are likely to impair the physical, mental or moral development of minors, except where it is ensured, by selecting the time of the broadcast or by any technical measure, that minors in the area of transmission will not normally hear or see such broadcasts.

3. In addition, when such programmes are broadcast in unencoded form Member States shall ensure that they are preceded by an acoustic warning or are identified by the presence of a visual symbol throughout their duration.

Article 28
1. Without prejudice to other provisions adopted by the Member States under civil, administrative or criminal law, any natural or legal person, regardless of nationality, whose legitimate interests, in particular reputation and good name, have been damaged by an assertion of incorrect facts in a television programme must have a right of reply or equivalent remedies. Member States shall ensure that the actual exercise of the right of reply or equivalent remedies is not hindered by the imposition of unreasonable terms or conditions. The reply shall be transmitted within a reasonable time subsequent to the request being substantiated and at a time and in a manner appropriate to the broadcast to which the request refers.

The approaches to editorial content taken by the Communications Act and the AVMS Directive demonstrate key differences. The Communications Act's approach is to set out, in great detail, the ways in which 'adequate protection' is to be provided, and assumes such comprehensive protection is both desirable and possible. The editorial requirements under the AVMS Directive provide a minimal baseline. There are no rules, for example, in relation to privacy and impartiality. The AVMS Directive does, however, contribute definitions and terminology that set out the criteria for determining whether material is subject to regulation and are therefore worth examining.

The Directive applies to any 'audiovisual media service'. It explains this is a service

> *which is under the editorial responsibility of a media service provider and the principal purpose of which is the provision of programmes in order to inform, entertain or educate, to the general public by electronic communications networks.*

Such a service is either (i) '"television broadcasting" or "television broadcast" (i.e. a linear audiovisual media service)' which is 'an audiovisual media service provided by a media service provider for simultaneous viewing of programmes on the basis of a programme schedule'. Or it is (ii) an '"on-demand audiovisual media service" (i.e. a non-linear audiovisual media service)' which is *an audiovisual media service provided by a media service provider for the viewing of programmes at the moment chosen by the user and at his individual request on the basis of a catalogue of programmes selected by the media service provider.*

Full meanings for programmes (a set of moving images), editorial responsibility (effective control for the selection and scheduling or cataloguing of programmes), and media service providers (the natural or legal person who has editorial responsibility) are also given.

The Directive contains references to the familiar world of 'television broadcasting', but the definitions themselves are notable in beginning to move us towards a platform-neutral world of 'audiovisual media services' that are either scheduled or (as we shall see below in relation to video on demand material) catalogued. These might appear rather dry and legalistic terms compared with the familiar world of 'telly', but as we increasingly consume content across the boundaries of broadcasting and online, definitions of scheduled and catalogued material provide a useful approach to defining content and applicable regulation.

In addition to the Communications Act and the AVMS Directive, the Broadcasting Code makes clear that the rules have been drafted in light of Human Rights Act 1998 and the European Convention on Human Rights. In particular the Broadcasting Code refers to the right of freedom of expression in Article 10 of the Convention (which includes the broadcasters' right to impart information and ideas as well as the audience's right to receive them), and to the right to a person's private and family life, home, and correspondence enshrined in Article 8, to freedom of thought, conscience, and religion in Article 9, and to the enjoyment of human rights without discrimination on grounds such as sex, race, and religion set out in Article 14.

3.2. Due impartiality requirements across broadcast services

In protecting members of the public from 'offensive and harmful material', the Communications Act pays special attention to the requirements of 'due impartiality'. Due impartiality is not required by the European and other legislation referred to above, it is a requirement elected under the Act. And it is a key distinguishing feature between broadcast and print journalism. As we shall see, its continuing survival as a requirement across standards regulation for television and radio is subject to vigorous debate. But what is 'due impartiality', and when and how do its requirements kick in?

The formulation of the Act draws on legal requirements that have existed from the inception of independent television. In his 2007 report on impartiality for the BBC Trust, *From Seesaw to Wagon Wheel: Safeguarding Impartiality in the 21st Century*,[28] John Bridcut reflected on the history of broadcasting regulation, particularly in relation to impartiality. He noted:

> *It was the new infant, ITV, that was first given a legislative rulebook in respect of content. When it was set up in 1955, the legislation aimed to ensure that public service broadcasting as devised by the BBC was not destroyed by commercial pressures. Impartiality was imposed by law on the new ITV companies. The Television Act of 1954 required ITV to exercise 'due impartiality' (which was taken to mean a level of impartiality appropriate*

---

[28] http://www.bbc.co.uk/bbctrust/assets/files/pdf/review_report_research/impartiality_21century/report.pdf.

to the nature and context of the programme) in news and on 'matters of political or industrial controversy or relating to current public policy'.

This formulation – the focus of impartiality on party politics and industrial disputes (discussed further below) – has been the basis for the regulation of impartiality ever since. It is a key requirement, alongside due accuracy in news and a requirement that factual programmes must not materially mislead the audience, placed on all broadcast journalists.

Commonly understood as a protection against bias,[29] the scope of the requirements in relation to impartiality are outlined in great detail in the Act. Section 319(2)(c) and (d) set out the objectives 'that news in television and radio services is presented with due impartiality' and is 'reported with due accuracy'. The Act also devotes the whole of Section 320 to 'special impartiality requirements' which apply to 'matters of political or industrial controversy' and 'matters relating to current public policy'. Broadcast coverage of such matters in news and other programmes (further defined as matters 'where politicians, industry and/or the media are in debate') must be duly impartial and must exclude the 'views or opinions' of the service provider (or, in the case of local services, ensure those views and opinions are not unduly prominent).

The application of impartiality rules only to political and industrial matters (outside of news programming) was a matter of contention before the advent of current Communications Act. In their 2002 paper *New News, Old News*,[30] an ITC and BSC research publication, Ian Hargreaves and James Thomas (whose key recommendations are explored below in Chapter 9) expressed concern about the focus of the impartiality rules on party politics and industrial disputes which were found to be of declining interest, particularly amongst young and minority audiences. They supported arguments in an IPPR paper[31] that 'in a time of diminished party loyalties, impartiality should be more broadly defined, to require that broadcasters provide even-handed treatment of issues of race, science, environment, health and any other matter of public controversy'. The BBC has recently taken this very course, and extended its application of impartiality, as discussed below.

In relation to those broadcasters other than the BBC who fall under Ofcom's rules on impartiality, the Broadcasting Code explains that due impartiality may be achieved within a single programme or over a series of 'editorially linked' programmes that allows for a single viewpoint to be expressed in a programme as long as a linked programme or linked programmes aimed at a like audience within an appropriate period of time achieve the impartiality requirements. If the subject is a 'major' matter of political or industrial controversy or public policy (explained as 'of national and often international importance') then 'an appropriately wide range of views must be included and given due weight in each programme or in clearly linked and timely programmes'.

These legislative requirements translate into section 5 of the Broadcasting Code which prefaces its rules with a definition of 'due impartiality'. It says:

> *'Due' is an important qualification to the concept of impartiality. Impartiality itself means not favouring one side over another. 'Due' means adequate or appropriate to the subject and nature of the programme. So 'due impartiality' does not mean an equal division of time has to be given to every view, or that every argument and every facet of every argument has to be represented.*

---

[29] www.bbc.co.uk/bbctrust/assets/files/pdf/our_work/editorial_guidelines/2010/audience_research.pdf.
[30] http://www.cardiff.ac.uk/jomec/resources/news.pdf.
[31] D. Tambini and J. Cowling (eds), *New News: Impartial Broadcasting in the Digital Age* (London: IPPR, 2002).

> *The approach to due impartiality may vary according to the nature of the subject, the type of programme and channel, the likely expectation of the audience as to content, and the extent to which the content and approach is signalled to the audience.*

Interestingly this meaning was prefaced by another sentence when originally drafted: 'Impartiality requires fairness, accuracy and an appropriate level of objectivity and even-handedness of approach to a subject.' However, following consultation in 2004, Ofcom accepted that the concepts of 'accuracy' and 'fairness' should not be mixed with 'impartiality' and dropped the references to both these and to 'objectivity' and instead developed the idea of 'even-handedness'.[32]

In addition to section 5 of the Code, sections 9 and 10 further secure the editorial independence of news programmes. Section 9, that covers commercial references in television programming, prohibits sponsorship of, or product placement in, news and current affairs programmes.[33] Similarly, section 10 on commercial communications in radio programmes, prohibits any commercial references, or material that implies a commercial arrangement in or around news bulletins. Factual programmes must also adhere to rule 2.2: 'Factual programmes or items or portrayals of factual matters must not materially mislead the audience'.

In relation to members of the public, or organisations, who are participants in, or the subject of, programmes, section 7 of the Broadcasting Code details the rule and practices to be followed in relation to fair treatment (including an opportunity to respond to allegations) and section 8 details the rule and practices to be followed to prevent any infringement of privacy in the making or broadcast of a programme unless it is warranted. It explains, for example, that 'if the reason is that it is in the public interest, then the broadcaster should be able to demonstrate that the public interest outweighs the right to privacy'.

In sum, outside of news programming where they are always required to satisfy the demands of due impartiality, the requirements kick in when the matters under discussion are politically or industrially controversial and/or relate to current public policy. Broadly, the more controversial the issue, the wider the range of views that may be appropriate in order to comply with the rules. However, whether matters are controversial or related to current public policy (i.e. whether the rules apply to any given material) is a matter of regulatory judgement, illustrated in the following case study.

Ofcom Case Study: The Great Global Warming Swindle Channel 4

Ofcom's fortnightly *Broadcast Bulletin*[34] reports on investigations into alleged breaches of the Ofcom Broadcasting Code and illuminates Ofcom's approach to the regulation of broadcast journalism. In *Bulletin* 114 (21 July 2008), sandwiched between a notice of sanction (£17,500) imposed on Square 1 Management Ltd in relation to the broadcast of sexually explicit material and complaints about product placement in *American Idol*, is an adjudication on Channel 4's *The Great Global Warming Swindle*.[35]

This documentary took an uncompromisingly polemical tone and set out to demonstrate that the argument that human activity was the cause of climate change was 'lies'. The opening of the programme set out its stall: 'Everywhere, you are told that man-made climate change is proved beyond doubt ... but you are being told lies'; 'it [the programme]

---

[32] http://stakeholders.ofcom.org.uk/binaries/consultations/Broadcasting_code/statement/261004_new.pdf.
[33] As discussed below, this prohibition is softened in relation to acquired news programming that may be simulcast live: http://stakeholders.ofcom.org.uk/binaries/broadcast/guidance/831193/section9.pdf.
[34] http://stakeholders.ofcom.org.uk/enforcement/broadcast-bulletins.
[35] http://stakeholders.ofcom.org.uk/binaries/enforcement/broadcast-bulletins/obb114/issue114.pdf.

is the story of the distortion of a whole area of science'; and 'it is a story about Westerners, invoking the threat of climatic disaster, to hinder vital industrial progress in the developing world'. The programme received 265 complaints, including a group complaint from a number of scientists, and its compliance with the requirements of accuracy and impartiality was investigated by Ofcom.

Ofcom's finding expressed concerns about the programme's 'intemperate' and 'aggressive' tone and about 'the portrayal of factual matters and omission of facts or views'. However it concluded that in relation to factual accuracy:

> it is important, in line with freedom of expression, that broadcasters are able to challenge current orthodoxy. It is self-evident that there will be strong disagreements over the 'facts' on an issue such as the causes of global warming – where some scientists disagree. Some may wish to challenge the evidence and the conclusions drawn from it. Channel 4, however, had the right to show this programme provided it remained within the Code and— despite certain reservations—Ofcom has determined that it did not ... materially mislead the audience so as to cause harm or offence.

In relation to due impartiality Ofcom first set out to establish whether the programme contained subject matter requiring the application of the due impartiality rules, i.e. it asked whether the programme contained 'matters of political or industrial controversy and matters relating to current public policy', which are explained in the Broadcasting Code as 'political or industrial issues on which politicians, industry and/or the media are in debate'. It held that the consensus view

> of human activity as the major cause of global warming does not appear to be challenged by any of the established political parties or other significant domestic or international institutions. Therefore, in this case, Ofcom considers that the subject matter of Parts One to Four of the programme (i.e. the scientific theory of man-made global warming) was not a matter of political or industrial controversy or a matter relating to current public policy. Having reached this view, it follows that the rules relating to the preservation of due impartiality did not apply to these parts. It is important to note that by simple virtue of the fact that one small group of people may disagree with a strongly prevailing consensus on an issue does not automatically make that issue a matter of controversy as defined in legislation and the Code and therefore a matter requiring due impartiality to be preserved.

In the closing section of the programme, however, Ofcom noted that the programme discussed the consequences of assuming that global warming was man-made, and specifically that it considered the policies followed by the UN and Western governments in the developing world. Policies in Africa were highlighted, through which Western governments were said to be seeking to limit industrial development and the use of fossil fuels by developing nations. Ofcom concluded that these were controversial matters that required due impartiality to be achieved: 'These issues are matters of major political controversy and are major matters relating to current public policy as defined by the Code' and that 'During this section no alternative views on this issue were presented.' It therefore found this part of the programme in breach of the Broadcasting Code's impartiality requirements. Ofcom also upheld related complaints of unfair treatment and directed Channel 4 to broadcast summaries of its adjudications.

The findings are useful in demonstrating the significance of the strength of the prevailing consensus in relation to decisions around due impartiality. Ofcom concluded that most of the programme, albeit polemical and backed by the views of only a small group of scientists who denied associations between human activity and global warming, did not trigger the requirements of impartiality. The programme portrayed the consensus around human activity being the major cause of global warming as 'lies', but for Ofcom the strength of that very consensus meant there was no obligation on the broadcaster to reflect other viewpoints. Only where the programme strayed into the territory of public policy was it found in breach of the Broadcasting Code.

The example of *The Great Global Warming Swindle* is therefore instructive in illustrating the limits of due impartiality. A programme widely perceived as 'controversial' in accompanying reviews, and by complainants, did not deal with 'controversial' issues as interpreted by Ofcom under the Broadcasting Code's definition. 'Impartiality' is commonly associated with 'broadcasting' as a whole. In fact due impartiality is a requirement in significant areas of broadcasting, but not in all areas, nor even (as demonstrated above) in all areas of current affairs broadcasting. The current imperative for the public to be *protected* from broadcasting 'favouring one side over another' depends on a range of contexts including whether there is considered to be consensus around a particular subject. We may ask, however, whether 'protection' is the most helpful starting point. Or whether citizens could and should have access to a public space in which there is a range of provision, over a range of platforms including broadcast media, that includes content where impartiality requirements apply, and are understood to apply, but also content where impartiality requirements do not apply and, importantly, are understood not to apply.

3.3. A pragmatic approach to international news services

Not only are the requirements of due impartiality limited in their scope to political and industrial matters, they are also limited in their application to increasingly globalised services. In the *New News, Old News*[36] research paper referred to above, Ian Hargreaves and James Thomas identified the emergence of '"diasporic television", meaning television consumed by an ethnic diaspora' and observed that it

> is potentially a very significant change in the character of broadcasting, which has previously been associated with strongly protected national jurisdictions. It is a moot point whether these services are, in practice, subject to a degree of regulatory scrutiny comparable with that which applies to mainstream UK television news services.

The link between news programming and due impartiality is fundamental to the Act and the Broadcasting Code as we have seen. However the ITC took a pragmatic approach to channels aimed at non-UK audiences, though licensed in the UK, leading Hargreaves and Thomas to argue:

> If the UK is to hold, across the board, to its standards about the due impartiality and accuracy of broadcast news, it should, logically, apply them as strenuously to non-UK news channels such as Fox News, Al Jazeera and

---

[36] http://www.cardiff.ac.uk/jomec/resources/news.pdf.

Zee TV, which are licensed for transmission within Britain. Apart from the practical difficulties involved in monitoring such a wide variety of channels in a multitude of languages, there is the tricky question of jurisdiction. At present, the ITC has the power and the ability to revoke the licences of all these broadcasters, but alternative web-based transmission mechanisms challenge this authority.

As demonstrated by the following case study, increasingly globalised content provision challenges national regulatory regimes. American services, for example, arise from a market-led regulatory framework where very different rules and enforcement practices apply.

United States: the fairness doctrine

Media regulation in the United States makes a similar broad distinction between broadcasting, print and the internet to that underpinning regulation in the UK, and supports the same philosophy that media should be independent of government. However it takes a very different approach to the role of the market in the regulation of content.

All American media are protected by the First Amendment to the Constitution which states that Congress shall make no law 'abridging the freedom of speech or of the press'.[37] Newspapers and the internet are not subject to statutory regulation although spectrum scarcity has, with similar historic justification to the UK, underpinned standards requirements imposed on broadcasting.

The Federal Communications Commission (FCC) licenses and regulates television, radio and telecommunications. Interestingly, as Robert McKenzie notes,[38]

the primary oversight body for the FCC is Congress, through the Senate Committee on Commerce, Science and Transportation, and the House Committee on Energy and Commerce. Both of these committee designations make clear the view of media primarily as an activity of commerce.

It is the commercial rather than cultural aspect to the media that underpins its regulation, and the approach of the FCC is to allow the market to regulate media content, providing limited intervention where the public demands. (A contrasting approach under which the cultural, rather than commercial, importance of the media is emphasised is discussed in Chapter 5 in relation to French media regulation.)

The FCC makes clear that 'in light of the fundamental importance of the free flow of information to our democracy, the First Amendment and the Communications Act bar the FCC from telling station licensees how to select material for news programs, or prohibiting the broadcast of an opinion on any subject'.[39] Two rules do relate specifically to journalism and regulate against hoaxes (the broadcast of false information concerning a crime or catastrophe) and news distortion. However, the bar is set very high in relation to breaching these rules. While the FCC states that 'rigging or slanting the news is a most heinous act against the public interest', it explains it would require documented evidence of intentional falsification or deliberate misrepresentation in order to investigate a station for news distortion. It goes on: 'In the absence of such documented evidence, the FCC has stressed that it cannot intervene.'

---

[37] http://www.house.gov/house/Constitution/Amend.html
[38] *Comparing Media Regulation Between France, the USA, Mexico and Ghana*, Robert McKenzie http://www.juridicas.unam.mx/publica/rev/comlawj/cont/6/arc/arc5.htm.
[39] http://transition.fcc.gov/mb/audio/decdoc/public_and_broadcasting.html.

Other rules include provision for access, and equality for broadcasts, relating to electoral candidates, and rules in relation to incitement to lawless action, the prohibition of obscene material, and a watershed for 'indecent or profane' programming.[40]

From 1949 the FCC imposed a 'fairness doctrine' requiring that 'public issues be presented by broadcasters and that each side of those issues be given fair coverage'.[41] This required broadcasters whose licences gave them access to, and influence over, audiences, to operate in the public interest both in the provision of programming about significant issues, and the presentation of that programming. However by the mid-1980s arguments had been successfully mounted that the fairness doctrine ran counter to rights of freedom of speech guaranteed by the First Amendment. In addition, the proliferation of television and radio stations provided access to the airwaves unimaginable at the time of the doctrine's inception, and provided a diversity of debate and comment across the channels. The doctrine was effectively abolished in 1987 under the Reagan administration (although not formally repealed by the FCC until August 2011 under the Obama administration). Those opposed to its abolition point to a coarsening of public debate: the damaging influence of conservative talk radio mediated by 'shock jocks' such as Rush Limbaugh, and the lack of restraint on channels like Fox News and such presenters as Sean Hannity and Glenn Beck. FCC guidance acknowledges:

> The FCC is caught in a tug-of-war between two consumer factions: on one side, consumers have urged the FCC to set guidelines to prevent bias or distortion by networks and station licensees or to supervise the gathering, editing and airing of news and comments; on the other side, consumers fear possible government intimidation or censorship of broadcast news operations.[42]

Although narrow limitations are placed on broadcasters (as set out above) the FCC makes it clear that its default position is a resolute bias against intervention:

> The Communications Act prohibits the FCC from censoring broadcast material. Additionally, the Communications Act and the First Amendment to the Constitution prohibit any action by the FCC that would interfere with free speech in broadcasting.

In response to the regulation of internationally originated content Ofcom, just as the ITC before it, has taken a pragmatic approach to services that are aimed at a non-UK audience. Fox News for example, may be simulcast on the Sky network. Ofcom guidance states:

> For those Ofcom licensees who are not broadcasting to the United Kingdom, the impartiality requirements still apply but the amount due may be less depending on the subject matter and the original country of reception.[43]

It takes a similarly pragmatic approach to product placement[44] which it prohibits in news programmes unless the following applies:

[40] http://transition.fcc.gov/mb/audio/decdoc/public_and_broadcasting.html.
[41] http://supreme.justia.com/us/395/367/case.html.
[42] http://www.fcc.gov/guides/broadcast-journalism-complaints.
[43] http://stakeholders.ofcom.org.uk/binaries/broadcast/guidance/831193/section5.pdf.
[44] Ofcom's Broadcast Code explains that product placement is 'The inclusion in a programme of, or of a reference to, a product, service or trade mark where the inclusion is for a commercial purpose, and is in return for the making of any payment, or the giving of other valuable consideration ...' http://stakeholders.ofcom.org.uk/broadcasting/broadcast-codes/broadcast-code/commercial-references-television.

In circumstances in which a broadcaster acquires news that is produced primarily for broadcast outside of the EU, we acknowledge that the broadcaster's ability to identify and cut out or obscure references to placed products, services and trade marks may be limited. This is particularly likely to be the case where live simulcasts are transmitted. In such cases, we expect that, where it is practically possible, broadcasters should take reasonable steps to determine whether the broadcast contains product placement and obscure or mask such placements.

Ofcom's expediency demonstrates a continuation of regulatory discretion in relation to news. It also serves to develop further questions over the fundamental principle of 'adequate protection' of the public in the Communications Act 2003 as set out above. Pragmatism over such simulcasts as Fox News, combined with access to online, print, and video on demand partial content, raises questions over how meaningful the current 'protections' are and will continue to be as global content and its availability develops.

3.4. Impartiality requirements

As we have seen from Bridcut's observations above, the demands for impartiality were originally linked to the provision of public service broadcasting and the purposes of those services were endorsed by the regulator through licences authorising each service. Today, however, these demands are made of an extraordinary range of licensees with radically different philosophies and viewpoints. Most significantly, those licensees with public service obligations adhere to the same code as the smallest commercial operators with no such duties. Chapter 10 seeks to argue that the current one-size-fits-all framework for broadcasting regulation fails to take account of the differences between providers with particular public duties and associated consumer expectations on the one hand, and private enterprises with no such duties on the other.

The proposed approach is to link the most rigorous regulatory standards to those providers of a public service (whether publicly or commercially owned or funded), and adopt a different approach towards private enterprises with purely commercial objectives. The consequences of such an approach, under which impartiality might not be a requirement for non-public service broadcasters, are illuminated in the following case study.

Ofcom case study: Press TV

Press TV is an Iranian international news network, which broadcasts in English, funded from advertising; Iranian tax-payers; technical and engineering sales; and sales from its archives. In *Bulletin* 139 (3 August 2009)[45] it was found to breach the Broadcasting Code's requirements for due impartiality.

(As an aside, just as in the first case study above, the full bulletin quickly demonstrates the range of Ofcom adjudications. It contained findings on a trailer for Playboy TV that contained 'adult sex' material and graphic sexual language; swearing in a reality show *Snoop Dogg's Father Hood* on 4 Music; and a complaint by Ray Mallon, mayor of Middlesbrough, that the community of Middlesbrough was unfairly portrayed as the worst place to live in the UK in a Channel 4 *Location, Location, Location* special.)

---

[45] http://stakeholders.ofcom.org.uk/enforcement/broadcast-bulletins/obb139.

Two Press TV programmes presented by Respect Party MP George Galloway, a weekly phone-in called *Comment* and a weekly current affairs programme *The Real Deal*, were the subject of complaints about bias against Israel. Ofcom found that the programmes were dealing with the subject of the Israeli military presence in Gaza in early 2009 and that this was a *major* political controversy which attracted the requirement for a wide range of significant views. This was not found to have been achieved. For example, in one phone-in programme George Galloway 'variously labelled Israel as committing: "murder"; "apartheid-style occupation"; "murder [of] UN employees"; and a "war crime"'. Ofcom found that:

> *There was not one telephone call from a pro-Israeli position in any of the programmes and only the most limited and short text or email messages from viewers from a pro-Israeli position.*

Galloway was also quoted as commenting 'Collectively punishing people is a Nazi tactic', that the Palestinians were under the 'iron heel of a brutal apartheid-style occupation', and as asking 'Which other country could murder United Nations employees?'

Ofcom did not take issue with the comments in relation to Nazi tactics and brutality, *per se*. It said it 'recognises that some people may strongly object to such views. However, the Code does not prohibit broadcasters from including such strongly-held views.' It also recognised:

> *that there is not, and should not be, any prohibition on broadcasters discussing controversial subjects. The Israeli–Palestinian conflict understandably raises extremely strong views and emotions from all sides. It is right that broadcasters are able to reflect such opinions within its programmes. There must be a place for such programming which gives air to highly opinionated and vocal reaction on issues of such importance. However, in order to comply with the Code, broadcasters must ensure that, when discussing matters of major political or industrial controversy or a major matter relating to current public policy, a real range of significant views are included in a programme. Further, in such cases, when presenting any significant alternative view, it must be given due weight and consideration.*

Ofcom considered that 'Alternative views in these programmes were not debated and/or discussed but dismissed and used as a further opportunity for the presenter to put forward his views.'

Bulletin 163 (2 August 2010)[46] found that Press TV had breached the Code with a 5 June programme *Remember Palestine* hosted by journalist Lauren Booth. This programme discussed the interception by Israeli military forces of a pro-Palestinian aid convoy in the Mediterranean in which Israeli commandos killed nine of the people aboard the convoy. Ofcom considered that the programme included a number of viewpoints, but all of them could be portrayed as being critical of the Israeli state's policy, in this case to use military force against the aid convoy which led to nine deaths. In relation to freedom of expression it said:

---

[46] http://stakeholders.ofcom.org.uk/enforcement/broadcast-bulletins/obb163.

It is important to note that the broadcasting of highly critical comments concerning the policies and actions of any one state (such as these here in this programme) is not, in itself, a breach of due impartiality

However the broadcaster did not ensure that alternative viewpoints were broadcast as required by the Broadcasting Code.

On 22 November 2010 Press TV was back in the Ofcom *Broadcast Bulletin* 170[47] when George Galloway's *Comment* programme was again found to have breached the due impartiality rules in programmes between 18 February and 24 June 2010. Ofcom was moved to take further action and concluded its adjudication:

In this case, alternative viewpoints were not adequately represented in the individual programmes or across the series as a whole. Ofcom remains concerned about Press TV's understanding and compliance processes in relation to Section Five of the Code. Therefore Press TV will be requested to attend a meeting with the regulator to explain and discuss its compliance processes further in this area.

In its response to Ofcom's investigation, Press TV accepted that its subject matter was a matter of political controversy but sought to argue that it had complied with the due impartiality rules. However, following publication of the adjudication Press TV accused Ofcom of censorship and sought to argue that the impartiality rules did not apply.[48]

In its news release Press TV accepted that the programme was biased, stating: 'Of course it was. How could it help but be biased?' But it claimed that rules on due impartiality only applied to news programming (where it accepted both sides of an issue must be reported). In relation to this programme it argued:

Remember, we are talking about a program showcasing Palestinian and pro-Palestinian views on various events. This particular episode was about the flotilla incident, so it should come as no surprise that the guests would express pro-Palestinian views.

In fact, the program makes no bones about the views expressed on it. To start out with, there's the title, Remembering Palestine. That, in itself, is a dead giveaway if ever there was one. Let's just say the viewer doesn't have to be 'Paul, the Octopus' to figure out which side the guests on the show will take. Let's face it.

If we heard of a program called, Remembering the Chalutzim (Israeli pioneers) or The Life and Times of David Ben Gurion, what would we think the show was about? Would we be surprised if it recounted Arab–Israeli conflicts from an Israeli perspective? In fact, wouldn't we be kind of shocked if it didn't? Would we expect the guests on the show to be Arabs, telling their side of the story?

Press TV's news release provides an unvarnished demonstration of its recognition of its output's 'bias' together with its argument that, so long as a provider wears its bias on its sleeve, the audience does not need to be 'protected' from the views expressed. Ofcom's

[47] http://stakeholders.ofcom.org.uk/binaries/enforcement/broadcast-bulletins/obb170/issue170.pdf.
[48] http://www.presstv.ir/detail/138201.html.

continuing relationship with Press TV[49] provokes useful questions about the potential consequences of relaxing rules on impartiality, and how far opinion-driven content could be tolerated. It invites consideration of how far rules on, for example, a right of reply and prohibiting incitement to hatred based on race, sex, religion, or nationality would satisfy our expectations of non-public service broadcasting content, if impartiality requirements were narrowed to public service providers.

Meanwhile Professor Stewart Purvis points out that we should not be complacent in assuming the adherence of mainstream channels to the principle of impartiality. In his view the 2011 'Arab Spring' demonstrated how mainstream media could also be challenged over its approach:[50]

> *Watching Press TV I noticed the words 'Islamic Awakening' kept appearing as an on-screen strap over coverage of demos in Arab countries. I searched the Press TV website for those words and found this is the Iranian Government's way of claiming their involvement in the demos. Slightly sinister, but it's also worth remembering that ITV News had a similar strap calling the Egyptian demos 'Fight for Freedom' or some such phrase. One man's Freedom Fighter is another man's Islamic Awakener.*

In addition, as discussed below in Chapters 4–6, partial views can be accessed in the self-regulated world of print media, as minimally regulated video on demand content, or on unregulated online services. Press TV's YouTube channel,[51] for example, is entirely unregulated. It provides Press TV content within a video on demand service but, because it is run from Tehran, the service does not fall within the jurisdiction of ATVOD (explored in Chapter 5). We must therefore ask how meaningful the 'protection' afforded by the Ofcom Code continues to be for scheduled content.

Consumer research, discussed in Chapter 7, demonstrates the importance attached to impartiality, although there is scepticism over whether it is achieved. Research also reveals different consumer expectations between broadcasters, for example, in relation to impartiality requirements for different broadcasters. These differing expectations may support differentiated standards in the future. For example, the BBC's research *Taste Standards and the BBC*, published in June 2009,[52] found that consumer expectations of the BBC were markedly different to those of other broadcasters:

> *Generally, the public expected – and received – higher standards from the BBC than from other broadcasters. 55% of people felt the BBC should lead the pack in relation to standards. This is very much in line with previous research into a number of different areas related to taste and standards (eg. Professor Sonia Livingstone's Literature Review[53]), with BBC One expected to be the 'gold standard' in terms of all broadcast channels.*

[49] In Mar. 2011 the *Guardian* reported that Press TV was found not to have breached the harm and offence rules of the Broadcasting Code when it broadcast a programme that showed an Iranian woman, Sakineh Ashtiani, participating in the reconstruction of her alleged part in the murder of her husband. The complaint was brought by a human rights activist Fazel Hawramy who questioned Press TV's access to Ms Ashtiani 'while she herself has been denied access to her lawyer': http://www.guardian.co.uk/media/2011/mar/23/ofcom-iranian-tv-murder-reconstruction. On 23 May 2011 Ofcom's Broadcast Bulletin upheld fairness and privacy complaints by Mr Maziar Bahari, a journalist interviewed by Press TV 'under duress' in an Iranian prison, breaches regarded as so serious the Ofcom 'will therefore consider whether this case warrants the imposition of a sanction': http://stakeholders.ofcom.org.uk/binaries/enforcement/broadcast-bulletins/obb182/obb182.pdf. On 14 Oct. 2011 the *Guardian* reported that Ofcom was deciding whether, following an opportunity for Press TV to submit a final appeal, to terminate Press TV's licence. http://www.guardian.co.uk/media/2011/oct/14/iran-press-tv-royal-family-off-air?newsfeed=true
[50] Email comments May 2011.
[51] http://www.youtube.com/user/PressTVGlobalNews.
[52] http://www.bbc.co.uk/aboutthebbc/reports/pdf/taste_standards_june2009.pdf.
[53] http://www.bbc.co.uk/aboutthebbc/reports/pdf/taste_standards_lit_review.pdf.

Similarly research conducted as part of Ofcom's 2008 Public Service Broadcasting Review[54] found the highest expectations were attached to the BBC, derived from its funding via the licence fee and perceived responsibilities to set standards. It observed: 'The BBC remains the cornerstone of [public service broadcasting], and expectations of the BBC are higher than they were in 2003 across a range of issues on standards and types of programming.' It also identified different expectations between the five main television channels (on whom public service content commitments are placed) and other channels.

Interestingly, the research found that audiences identified public service qualities in channels that have no public service responsibilities and observed:

> Some commercial digital channels have small loyal audiences for whom the channel fulfils a need and are seen to deliver 'PSB [public service broadcasting] type' content. Single genre commercial channels (most notably The Discovery Channel, UKTV History and Sky News) were rated very highly among their viewers across PSB purposes.

Audience expectations of Sky News are particularly interesting. Consideration of any relaxation to impartiality requirements includes questions around impartiality requirements for news. Channel 4 has argued[55] that impartiality rules should be retained for public service broadcasting (PSB) and non-PSB UK TV news providers, largely because of the dominance of Sky News. It argued that the broadcast environment is very different to the newspaper market:

> impartiality rules provide the bedrock upon which all standards in UK TV news broadcasting are built, and so the rules should be retained for non-PSB licensed UK TV news suppliers too (e.g. Sky News). Given that virtually 100 per cent of TV news viewing in the UK is to programmes provided either by the BBC, the commercial PSBs or Sky, relaxation of the impartiality rules for non-PSB TV providers would effectively create a single, potential partial news supplier – Sky News. If, in this scenario, Sky News were to adopt a particular political agenda (whether left or right) it would leave one or more political parties without any voice in the TV news market. This would represent a very different situation to the one which exists in the newspaper market. In light of the massive explosion in choice and opinion that is being facilitated by the internet, which is not regulated for impartiality, Channel 4 would suggest that there is little reason currently to deregulate TV news in this way.

Looking at the debate more broadly it argued:

> impartiality is a core regulatory function in UK broadcasting regulation. All content regulation will become increasingly difficult to justify as regulated services exist side by side with unregulated ones, but this does not mean that it will be unenforceable for licensed services. Indeed, it is likely that the fact that a service is licensed, and therefore regulated, will become a valuable sign of trustworthiness for consumers. Arguably, with a plethora of news sources, it is ever more important for viewers to be able to identify who it is they can trust for an objective view.

---

[54] http://stakeholders.ofcom.org.uk/binaries/consultations/psb2_1/annexes/annex6.pdf.
[55] http://stakeholders.ofcom.org.uk/binaries/research/tv-research/responses.pdf.

While Channel 4 argued that Sky News would be peculiarly advantaged by removing the rules on impartiality from all non-PSB providers, under the proposals here it would be open to all providers, including Sky News, to differentiate their content and attract audiences and online users by voluntarily adopting this regulation. This could prove attractive to Sky News, having built up a brand and audience based on impartial news coverage, indeed Ofcom's 2008 Public Service Broadcasting review commented on the higher levels of trust in Sky News compared to levels of trust in other channels, with Sky News viewers describing it 'as having "social value" and offering high quality content'.[56]

Should impartiality requirements for news be removed, a key concern is that it would be open to new or existing news providers to follow a Fox News route, resulting in news provision across UK media being cheapened as a result, and public debate diminished. However, as we have seen in the discussion of regulation in the United States above, the American context in which Fox News is delivered is very different to that in the UK. Not only are there no impartiality requirements for news or matters of public debate, there are also no equivalent accuracy requirements, and the bar for proving distortion of news is set extremely high.

This report invites consideration of the extent to which a plurality of impartial and partial content, underpinned by transparency as a guarantor of informed public choices, should be promoted across platforms and, if so, whether those news services without public service obligations should be released from impartiality requirements. As we shall see, while there are no impartiality requirements for the newspaper industry, there is a requirement to maintain a clear distinction between fact and opinion. Rules provide against 'inaccurate, misleading or distorted information' and require a distinction to be made between 'comment, conjecture and fact'.[57] Building on this, an alternative approach to requiring 'protection' from bias on all broadcast services could be to place the onus on 'enabling' the consumer of regulated services to distinguish between impartial and partial providers, to distinguish facts from opinions, and to be entitled to expect content does not materially mislead. Chapter 10 proposes a framework that would allow for and incentivise a rich diversity of news providers, both impartial and partial, supported by commitments in relation to accuracy and misleadingness. A broadcast licence would no longer be relied on as the 'sign of trustworthiness' for the consumer referred to by Channel 4 above; instead a transparent regulatory framework would make requirements easily identifiable by consumers across broadcast, print, video on demand, and online content.

3.5. A diverse domestic community challenges 'generally accepted standards'

In the first of the Press TV adjudications outlined above, Ofcom referred to the decision of its Content Sanctions Committee, 21 July 2007, to fine another broadcaster, Islam Channel Ltd, £30,000 for breaches of the rules on due impartiality and rules concerning candidates in UK elections, including a prohibition on them acting as programme presenters during the election period.[58] Islam Channel is a specialist religious channel that broadcasts on the Sky digital satellite platform and is directed at a largely Muslim audience in the UK. Its output ranges from religious instruction programmes to current affairs and documentary programmes.

In its sanction decision Ofcom made important observations about the contribution of the Islam Channel. It noted:

---

[56] http://stakeholders.ofcom.org.uk/binaries/consultations/psb2_1/annexes/annex6.pdf.
[57] http://www.pcc.org.uk/cop/practice.html.
[58] http://www.ofcom.org.uk/tv/obb/ocsc_adjud/islamchannel.pdf.

the special remit of the Islam Channel to broadcast programmes from an Islamic perspective designed to appeal at the same time to a largely underserved domestic audience and to an international audience with very different expectations. Ofcom accepted that this created particular challenges for compliance.

In addition:

Ofcom did not underestimate the importance of the Islam Channel in providing a platform for different views. Ofcom considered that it was important to ensure that the plurality of viewpoints and broadening of the debate on key issues facing society that a channel like the Islam Channel can provide was not discouraged.

However, while Ofcom applauded the fact that the principle of a 'plurality of viewpoints' *across* broadcasting is furthered by the very existence of the Islam Channel, the lack of a range of viewpoints *within* the Channel's programming led to the impartiality finding in 2007, and related sanction. In 2010 another adjudication found that the Islam Channel was in breach of the Broadcasting Code in relation to due impartiality in its coverage of Israeli policies in Gaza.[59]

In the same *Bulletin* Ofcom found Islam Channel in breach of harm and offence requirements in the Broadcasting Code. It noted that 'Islam Channel transmitted various programmes aimed at an Islamic audience, which included interpretations and analysis of Islamic law and teaching on a range of issues'. The service contributed to the diverse range of programming across the broadcasting spectrum, and catered for what Ofcom recognises to be an underserved domestic audience. However, with that very diversity came viewpoints found to be offensive under the Broadcasting Code, as illustrated in the following case study.

Ofcom case study: Islam Channel
In *Bulletin* 169[60] (8 November 2010) editions of two programmes were found in breach of the Broadcasting Code in relation to harm and offence. These were *IslamiQa*, a phone-in programme where viewers pose the presenter questions, by telephone, asking for religious-based advice on a range of issues and *Muslimah Dilemma*, a discussion programme considering issues from an Islamic perspective.

In the *IslamiQa* phone-in on 18 May 2008 a female caller asked 'If your husband is hitting you, do you have the right to hit him back?' The presenter offered the following advice:

as far as the hitting is concerned, in Islam we have no right to hit the woman in a way that damages her eye or damages her tooth or damages her face or makes her ugly. Maximum what you can do, you can see the pen over here, in my hand, this kind of a stick can be used just to make her feel that you are not happy with her. That's the only maximum that you can do, just to make her understand. Otherwise your husband has no right to hit you that way and at the same time even if he has done that, may Allah forgive him.

---

[59] http://stakeholders.ofcom.org.uk/binaries/enforcement/broadcast-bulletins/obb169/issue169.pdf.
[60] http://stakeholders.ofcom.org.uk/enforcement/broadcast-bulletins/obb169.

In its finding Ofcom noted that the broadcaster argued that 'it is unjustifiable to hit a woman which could in any way cause any harm, damage or pain', and that the presenter demonstrated this point by tapping his own hand with a pen 'as a comparison to the "Siwaak" which is a light twig'.

However Ofcom considered that the presenter gave:

> advice to viewers that it was permissible for a husband to physically punish his wife, even though according to the broadcaster it was to be only in certain circumstances, and undertaken with restraint, and even if the language used by the presenter could be perceived by some as relatively mild. In Ofcom's opinion, the advocacy of any form of violence (however limited), as happened in this particular case, is not acceptable and would be offensive to many in the audience.

In *Muslimah Dilemma* on 12 April 2009 a guest interviewee made the following comments:

> And really the idea that a woman cannot refuse her husband's [sexual] relations – this is not strange to a Muslim because it is part of maintaining that strong marriage. In fact it is a bit strange, the converse is strange. To refuse relations would harm a marriage.
>
> But it shouldn't be such a big problem where the man feels he has to force himself upon the woman because the understanding should be created within the system through the implementation of all the laws of Islam, that ... marriage is about seeking tranquillity, it's about harmony that should be in the mind of the man and the woman alike.

Ofcom noted that during the discussion the interviewee 'made a number of points which could be portrayed as encouraging husbands and wives to treat each other with respect' and that she was 'talking against the back-drop of legislative changes in Afghanistan, and the reaction of Western media to these legislative changes'. However Ofcom considered that:

> the views expressed in the programme concerning marital relations might have suggested to many in the audience that it would be permissible for a husband to oblige his wife to have sexual relations against her will, whether or not he used some form of threat of violence. This would have had the potential to cause offence.

Concluding its findings, Ofcom requested a meeting with Islam Channel:

> Ofcom remains concerned about Islam Channel's understanding and compliance processes in relation to the Code. This is particularly the case, given that the Islam Channel has previously been fined for breaches of the Code relating to 'due impartiality'.

These case studies, in relation to harm and offence, again invite us to consider the type of material that could be permitted should the current regulations in these areas be removed or significantly relaxed. Chapter 10 considers how far 'harmful' and 'offensive' content should be distinguished from each other and, as discussed above in relation to impartiality, how meaningful 'protection' afforded by the Ofcom Code continues to be in the context of the range of content accessible across platforms.

3.6. Digital switchover challenges the traditional licensing of spectrum

The licensing of spectrum, as discussed in Chapter 2, has provided the foundations on which standards requirements have been built. It has enabled statutory intervention (justified by the need to allocate a limited resource), and provided leverage (allowing standards requirements to be attached to spectrum access). It underpins the penalties that follow from breaching these standards requirements, including publication of a finding in Ofcom's *Broadcast Bulletin*, the imposition of a fine, or ultimately the power to revoke a licence, meaning that if the licensee continues to provide the relevant service they are guilty of a criminal offence.

With the move to digital switchover this regulatory leverage diminishes, causing Professor Stewart Purvis in his 2010 RTS Fleming Lecture discussed in Chapter 9 to 'call time on analogue regulation' because 'technology now allows so many more players to reach audiences within spectrum and without spectrum'. 'Within spectrum' we have moved from competition for the scarce resource that is analogue spectrum to digital capacity that exceeds take-up by channels. Ofcom's *Communications Market Report* published in 2010[61] reported that the number of television channels broadcasting in the UK had declined for the first time, from 495 at the end of 2008 to 490 in 2009. While the report explained that there are some constraints on providers, for example, the Sky Digital satellite platform cannot further increase the number of standard definition channels, it concluded that: 'the contraction in the number of channels could suggest that the multichannel market is reaching saturation point'. Leverage linked to spectrum is also challenged from 'without' by the potential for alternative, or complementary, online services.

Such challenges to the natural order of licensing and regulation force us to divorce regulatory practices from regulatory purposes, and invite us to rethink the justification for regulation. While the licensing of spectrum has provided a mechanism for the regulation of broadcast content, there is a wider justification, based on democratic value, in the provision of regulated public space. As Stephen Whittle observed:

> *The difficulty is the traditional argument has been about access to spectrum, whereas here you're not talking about what has been up to now a scarce resource, but you are still saying public space ... Broadly speaking those people who seek a place in the public space have to abide by certain rules about how debate is conducted.*[62]

How we view this 'public space', and the value of access to it, lies at the heart of this report's recommendations which propose a regulated public space across platforms. Chapter 10 also considers the 'notification' system under ATVOD, in which 'on-demand' services are not licensed but instead notify the authority of their intention to provide a service and are then subject to associated regulation. It considers the potential for considering this model for 'scheduled' services.

---

[61] http://stakeholders.ofcom.org.uk/binaries/research/cmr/753567/CMR_2010_FINAL.pdf.
[62] Interview May 2011.

It is notable that for radio the timetable for digital switchover is very much more extended. Matt Payton of RadioCentre, the trade organisation representing commercial radio, argues that standards regulation is not therefore as high a priority for commercial radio as other commercial concerns. In addition, consumption is still based largely around a dial, rather than the more active selection from an electronic programme guide:

> *You only need to look at the way the BBC has had to react to things on their radio output – Ross/Brand[63] being the most obvious – and you can see we're a long way from paring back harm and offence regulation in radio generally and I think that applies to commercial radio equally. There's still a listener expectation, and particularly the way radio is consumed still at the moment – it's on the school run, in the car, in the background when the kids are having breakfast. The consumption is still pushed rather than pulled and it's going to remain that way for the time being.[64]*

Chapter 10 proposes an approach that is consistent across commercial providers (television, radio, print, video on demand, or online) but supports providers in responding to the demands of different audiences.

3.7. Regulating BBC standards

Regulation of the BBC's standards combines external and self-regulation. Observance of the Ofcom Code is required of the BBC by the BBC Agreement, with exceptions (agreed under the Memorandum Of Understanding with Ofcom). So far, so simple. However the House of Lords Select Committee on Communications, *Inquiry into the Governance and Regulation of the BBC,* identified a complex web of regulatory responsibility as set out its report published in June 2011.[65]

Section 5 of Ofcom's Broadcasting Code (on Due Impartiality and Due Accuracy and Undue Prominence of Views and Opinions), and section 6 (on Elections and Referendums) do not apply to BBC services funded by the licence fee, which are instead regulated on these matters by the BBC Trust. Section 9 (on commercial references in television programming) does not apply to the BBC, except in relation to certain product placement rules, where it does apply. None of the provisions of the Broadcasting Code apply to the BBC World Service while it is funded by grant in aid, although this will change when the BBC takes on the responsibility for its funding in 2014. Meanwhile both the BBC and Ofcom provide complaints mechanisms in relation to harm and offence, fairness and privacy. Different arrangements arise in relation to video on demand material and print publications, and vary in relation to the BBC's commercial arm BBC Worldwide.

A table included in the Select Committee report, and annexed to this paper, identified a number of authorities including the BBC Trust, Ofcom, ATVOD and the PCC regulating, and at times duplicating regulation over, BBC content. A second table set out complaint mechanisms for non-BBC content and is also annexed to this paper. Their complexity illuminates the bewildering array of bodies with which both providers and consumers must negotiate. Of significant concern to the Committee in relation to the BBC was the general lack of transparency for consumers over which body to turn to with a complaint, and the particular issue of the regulation of impartiality and accuracy.

---

[63] Breaches of the Ofcom Broadcasting Code by *The Russell Brand Show* resulted in fines of £150,000 being imposed on the BBC: http://stakeholders.ofcom.org.uk/binaries/enforcement/content-sanctions-adjudications/BBCRadio2TheRussell-BrandShow.pdf.

[64] Interview May 2011.

[65] http://www.publications.parliament.uk/pa/ld201012/ldselect/ldcomuni/166/16602.htm.

It is the BBC Trust that commissions and approves the BBC's weighty editorial guidelines and supporting guidance. Nineteen sections of introductory notes, principles, and practices cover issues ranging from reporting anti-social behaviour through to interacting with audiences. However, one area is singled out as a defining characteristic of the BBC:

> *Impartiality lies at the core of the BBC's commitment to its audiences. We will apply due impartiality to all our subject matter and will reflect a breadth and diversity of opinion across our output as a whole, over an appropriate period, so that no significant strand of thought is knowingly unreflected or under-represented. We will be fair and open-minded when examining evidence and weighing material facts.*

By way of example, in the Trust's *Editorial Standards Committee Bulletin* of 3 March 2009, 113 pages of findings of the Committee were published in relation to complaints about BBC Middle East Editor Jeremy Bowen's *From Our Own Correspondent*, BBC Radio 4, 12 January 2008,[66] and a related online article 'How 1967 defined the Middle East'. Although not all the complaints were upheld, both were variously found not to have achieved accuracy and due impartiality. It was Bowen's reference in the online article to Zionism's 'innate instinct to push out the frontier' that received particular press attention.

In its finding the Trust explained that:

> *The Committee discussed the argument put forward by the BBC that, in this item, the Middle East Editor was offering his professional judgment about the events of 1967. The guideline says:*
>   *'our journalists and presenters, including those in news and current affairs, may provide professional judgments but may not express personal opinions on matters of public policy or political or industrial controversy. Our audiences should not be able to tell from BBC programmes or other BBC output the personal views of our journalists and presenters on such matters.'*
> *The Committee considered that a 'professional judgment' on a matter of opinion regarding a highly controversial subject should be contextualised to indicate that other views exist.*

The finding is interesting because, following it, Bowen's online article was BBC amended.[67] Although the amended piece is introduced as Jeremy Bowen's 'own assessment' it provides an insight into how wider accuracy and impartiality requirements were finally adhered to by comparison to the first publication.

BBC Trust case study: 'How 1967 Defined the Middle East'

Following the BBC Trust's adjudication of 3 March 2009, Jeremy Bowen's online article 'How 1967 Defined the Middle East' was amended to take account of its findings on accuracy and impartiality. Highlighted here in bold are the original and amended sections.

The original introduction ran 'To understand what is happening between Israel and the Palestinians now, it is important to understand what happened in the Middle East war of 1967'. Following the adjudication this was extended with the words ' – **a subject of much debate amongst historians**'.

---

[66] http://www.bbc.co.uk/bbctrust/assets/files/pdf/appeals/esc_bulletins/2009/mar.pdf.
[67] http://news.bbc.co.uk/1/hi/6709173.stm.

In the original piece Bowen wrote 'The myth of the 1967 Middle East war was that the Israeli David slew the Arab Goliath. It is more accurate to say there were two Goliaths in the Middle East.' Amended after the Trust finding it reads 'While historians hold different views on the 1967 war, one school of thought is that it is a myth to suggest the Israeli David slew the Arab Goliath, and that it is more accurate to say there were two Goliaths in the Middle East.'

The section of Bowen's original text which received most publicity when the finding was published ran as follows: 'When the messianic moment of victory combined with Zionism's innate instinct to push out the frontier, the result was the settlement movement.' Following the Trust's finding this was changed to 'When the messianic moment of victory combined with the tendency within Zionism to push out the frontier, the result was the settlement movement.'

And later 'Forty years on, Israel has settled around 450,000 people on land occupied in 1967, in defiance of everyone's interpretation of international law except its own' was changed to 'Forty years on, Israel has settled around 450,000 people on land occupied in 1967, in defiance of almost all countries' interpretation of international law except its own'.

The rewriting of Bowen's online comments also serves to illustrate the platform-neutral approach the BBC takes to its content, illustrated in the cross-platform guidance the BBC provides in its Editorial Guidelines. It demonstrates the connection between regulation and *brand* rather than *medium* to which we will return in Chapter 10. The BBC applies its regulatory framework (including the requirement for impartiality) across its content, including text-based online articles. Ofcom, on the other hand, applies the Broadcasting Code only to Ofcom licensees and not to their associated online content.

As noted above, impartiality lies 'at the core' of the BBC's declared commitment to its audiences. In October 2010, following a review of the BBC Editorial Guidelines some requirements were revised[68] and in the case of impartiality the requirements for 'due impartiality' across controversial subjects were extended. Alison Hastings, Chair of the Trust's Editorial Standards Committee, explained:

> *The most significant change from the 2005 edition concerns impartiality. The guideline has been extensively revised to take account, in particular, of the Bridcut report[69] on impartiality in the 21st century published by the Trust in 2007, but also of extensive feedback on the wording of this guideline as originally proposed. The new guideline makes clear that 'due impartiality' applies to all subjects covered by the BBC. This goes further than the duty of impartiality laid on the BBC by the Charter and Agreement. The new guideline also makes clear that achieving impartiality will often involve more than a simple balance between opposing viewpoints. The BBC must be inclusive, consider the broad perspective, and ensure that the existence of a range of views is appropriately reflected. In addition the new guideline extends the definition of 'controversial' subjects beyond those of public policy and political or industrial controversy to include controversy within religion, science, finance, culture, ethics and other matters.*

Thus the BBC elected to raise the bar in relation to standards of due impartiality required of its services and the rest of the broadcasting sector. It drew on audience research,

---

[68] http://www.bbc.co.uk/bbctrust/news/press_releases/2010/october/editorial_guidelines.shtml.
[69] *From Seesaw to Wagon Wheel: Safeguarding Impartiality in the 21st Century* www.bbc.co.uk/bbctrust/assets/files/pdf/review_report_research/impartiality_21century/report.pdf.

specifically commissioned to inform the guidelines, to explain its revisions. A couple of quotations were highlighted from the research[70] to illustrate audience expectations: '*I would expect the BBC to be stricter, more appropriate.*' (Female, 35–54, Manchester) and '*I'd say impartiality is much more important than offensiveness. If stuff is biased you may not realise it ...*' (Male, 35–54, Londonderry).

Similarly, the BBC's 2009 report, *Taste, Standards and the BBC* (see n. 52 above), reflected on the extensive research conducted into the standards it both achieves and aspires to:

> *Through it all, a clear sense emerges of what audiences expect of the BBC. They very explicitly want the BBC to be different from other broadcasters, to be a benchmark of quality and trust in all its output; but not so different that it drifts apart from the currency of public attitudes and fails to reflect audiences honestly back to themselves. They value creative innovation and the strong talents and personalities who capture the nation's sometimes outrageous sense of humour; but value equally the tough judgement and control that keeps fundamental standards in place even when material is strong or challenging.*

The BBC approach to its impartiality requirements is significant in that it creates clear blue water between itself and the rest of broadcasting in relation to extending the application of impartiality requirements. The case study on Channel 4's *The Great Global Warming Swindle* discussed above is pertinent. Other than one concluding issue on Western policy in the developing world, the programme was not found to breach Ofcom's impartiality rules. However, with the widening of the BBC's equivalent rules to subjects including science (discussed in *BBC Trust Review of Impartiality and Accuracy of the BBC's Coverage of Science* published in July 2011[71]) such a programme might not be broadcast on the BBC without balancing viewpoints (within the programme or in linked programmes) to achieve impartiality.

Consumer research, as discussed in Chapter 7, reveals that while the public sees impartiality as important, in particular in relation to television news, there is also public scepticism over whether impartiality can actually be achieved. This scepticism was shared in interviews for this report.

Stephen Whittle, who was responsible for overseeing a fundamental revision of BBC guidelines during his 2001–6 tenure as Controller Editorial Policy, noted the complexity attached to expectations around impartiality for all broadcasters including the BBC, commenting that the public 'will notice when the BBC celebrates England winning a match, or indeed the Royal Wedding' and that:

> *there's some scepticism over the ability to achieve [impartiality], because in the end the mere selection of stories, however even-handedly you present them, has its own judgement about what is most important. There's nothing to apologise for in exercising judgement, but it's not strictly speaking impartial.*[72]

Similarly, Stewart Purvis, as discussed above, commented on the lack of neutrality demonstrated by both Press TV and ITV in covering the 'Arab Spring'. Stephen Abell, Director of the Press Complaints Commission, argued that impartiality is an aspiration but muddies the waters as a regulatory requirement:

[70] http://www.bbc.co.uk/bbctrust/assets/files/pdf/our_work/editorial_guidelines/2010/audience_research.pdf.
[71] http://www.bbc.co.uk/bbctrust/assets/files/pdf/our_work/science_impartiality/science_impartiality.pdf.
[72] Interview May 2011.

> *Philosophically it's very difficult to say what impartiality means in practice – if you mean balance you should say balance. No one is impartial, it's a human impossibility to be impartial about anything, to say that a broadcaster doesn't colour their language, or colour their tone, in terms of what they select. You can't neutrally present anything. Therefore if you can't neutrally present it, what is the regulatory requirement? Now I understand the BBC prides itself on fairness and balance ... If we're talking about balance and fairness then we should say that's what we mean. I just don't believe in impartiality.*[73]

However, for the BBC there is a newly strengthened and widened association between impartiality and the BBC brand. As Michael Grade remarked, 'It's the BBC that keeps [the rest of] us honest'[74] and this decision may set competitive standards for the media industry as a whole. It also has the potential to create, or reinforce, a distinction for consumers between BBC and other broadcast content which may usefully presage the development of clearly differentiated public service content regulation discussed in Chapter 10.

On the other hand, however, a lack of transparency over differing impartiality requirements between the BBC and other providers (including other public service content providers); the duplication between Ofcom and Trust in areas of complaints oversight; and lack of clarity for the consumer over which aspects of the Ofcom Broadcasting Code do and do not apply to the BBC, have the potential to cause considerable consumer confusion. Chapter 10 considers how such differentiation may be built into a regulatory framework that is readily signalled to consumers and meaningful for providers.

---

[73] Interview May 2011.
[74] http://www.bbc.co.uk/pressoffice/speeches/stories/bpv_grade.shtml.

4. Newspaper Regulation

In contrast to the statutory regulation of radio and television, supported by the detailed rules and guidance discussed above and underpinned by sanctions linked to a system of licences, newspapers are self-regulated. 2011 has seen seismic criticism of the present self-regulatory arrangements. Time has been called on the body responsible for self-regulation, the Press Complaints Commission (PCC), and its chairman Baroness Buscombe announced her departure following a storm of criticism over the PCC's handling of the 'phone-hacking' scandal over a number of years.[75] Lord Justice Leveson's inquiry was charged by the Prime Minister with 'making recommendations for a new, more effective way of regulating the press'.[76] Debate immediately followed on whether voluntary self-regulation should be replaced by some form of statutory framework for the press.

However, before looking forward to a system that, in the Prime Minister's words, 'supports [press] freedom, plurality and independence from Government, but which also demands the highest ethical and professional standards', it is worth reviewing the recent history of press regulation. First, the history and development of the PCC, its membership, its philosophy of voluntary self-regulation, and the interplay between it and other regulators, all provide lessons that will be extremely valuable in informing and shaping future choices. Secondly, while its Code has been egregiously flouted by those involved in the phone-hacking scandal, the standards set out in the Code are widely valued and have shaped responses to a range of complaints and newspaper titles. Thirdly, the 'press' can no longer be understood as an easily identifiable medium. As discussed below, the PCC has expanded its remit to cover newspapers online, including extensive audiovisual material, services that are rapidly taking on the traditional look and feel of broadcasting, and including the blogs and tweets of their journalists. Future regulation of the press, as argued in this chapter, will have to find its place in this converged world.

In addition, as Director General of the BBC, Mark Thompson observed in an article on 27 July 2011:

> *The phone-hacking scandal has put investigative journalism in the dock. Yet without investigative journalism – and in particular the meticulous work of one investigative journalist, Nick Davies, of the Guardian – it's a scandal that would have never seen the light of day.*[77]

---

[75] http://www.pcc.org.uk/news/index.html?article=NzI4Mw==. On 13Oct. 2011 the PCC announced the appointment of Lord David Hunt as its new Chair http://www.pcc.org.uk/news/index.html?article=NzQwMA==

[76] http://www.publications.parliament.uk/pa/cm201011/cmhansrd/cm110713/debtext/110713-0001.htm.

[77] http://www.bbc.co.uk/blogs/theeditors/2011/07/investigative_journalism_in_th.html.

Or, in the words of James Harding, editor of *The Times*: 'Journalism is in the dock and journalism put it there.'[78] The Information Commissioner's Office 2006 report *What Price Privacy?*,[79] which found considerable evidence of 'the unlawful trade in confidential personal information', also acknowledged the contribution of investigative journalism when it referred to:

> *A Guardian report in September 2002 indicating a data 'black market' and highlighting a private detective agency which had been found to have sold information from police sources to the News of the World, Daily Mirror and Sunday Mirror. A Sunday Telegraph report in December 2002 that private detective agencies routinely tapped private telephone calls for the tabloid press, with some agencies deriving the bulk of their income from such work and such clients.*

Reform of the current regulation of the press will need to ensure that it in no way diminishes such significant reporting in any area. Tom Watson MP, a member of the Culture, Media and Sport Select Committee, although active in pursuing full exposure of the phone-hacking scandal, counselled that 'if you over-react to a crisis legislatively it generally ends in disaster'. He argued in an interview with the *Telegraph* on 22 July 2011:[80]

> *The future regulatory arrangements for the newspaper industry need to be done in a much calmer, deliberative way, in slower time when we've got beyond this media firestorm. I would like Parliament to restate the case for a self-regulatory model that would operate with sanctions that are effective rather than ones that editors can kind of dismiss.*

4.1. A self-regulatory body and slim voluntary code applies to newspapers and magazines

In contrast to the 134-page Ofcom Broadcasting Code,[81] the Editors' Code of Practice, with its 'clauses' not 'rules', fits onto just one side of A4[82] or can be provided as wallet-sized version. It is produced by the Society of Editors on behalf of the press and is enforced by the Press Complaints Commission. It declares it is designed to safeguard freedom of expression while addressing potentially competing rights such as privacy.[83] The clauses contained in the PCC Editors' Code are consistent with the approach of corresponding rules in the Ofcom Broadcasting Code. Where they differ is the far narrower scope of the Editors' Code. Most significantly while the Editors' Code seeks to bind its members to upholding minimum standards including fairness, accuracy, and privacy, it has no requirements over impartiality or harm and offence (in relation to adults or under-18s).

The first clause of the Editors' Code relates to accuracy and the care that must be taken 'not to publish inaccurate, misleading or distorted information, including pictures'. The partiality of the press is recognised as a given, in clause 1(iii), but is also linked to transparency for the consumer: 'The Press, whilst free to be partisan, must distinguish clearly between comment, conjecture and fact.'

---

[78] The Media Show Radio Four 27 July 2011 http://www.bbc.co.uk/programmes/b012r6v4.

[79] http://www.ico.gov.uk/~/media/documents/library/Corporate/Research_and_reports/WHAT_PRICE_PRIVACY.ashx.

[80] http://www.telegraph.co.uk/news/uknews/phone-hacking/8653960/Phone-Hacking-emails-next-scandal-says-Tom-Watson.html.

[81] http://stakeholders.ofcom.org.uk/binaries/broadcast/831190/broadcastingcode2011.pdf.

[82] http://www.pcc.org.uk/cop/practice.html.

[83] http://www.pcc.org.uk.

The PCC's background to the Editors' Code recognises the difference between press regulation and the regulation of broadcast media. It explains this in relation to 'taste and offence', though it is notably silent on the issue of 'harm':

> *The terms of the Editors' Code of Practice do not address issues of taste and offence. The Code is designed to address the potentially competing rights of freedom of expression and other rights of individuals, such as privacy. Newspapers and magazines have editorial freedom to publish what they consider to be appropriate provided that the rights of individuals – enshrined in the terms of the Code which specifically defines and protects these rights – are not compromised. To come to an inevitably subjective judgement as to whether such material is tasteless or offensive would amount to the Commission acting as a moral arbiter, which can lead to censorship. The issue of taste is an interesting demonstration of how press regulation differs from the way that other media are regulated. Advertising billboards (and to a lesser extent television programmes, for example), contain information disseminated on a very wide scale, the consumption of which cannot necessarily be controlled. As anyone can look at an advert, it is necessary to ensure that all advertisements do not break basic standards of decency and taste. On the other hand, newspapers are actively purchased and therefore need not be subject to the same restrictions.*

It continues:

> *The print media is fundamentally different from other media in the way it is transmitted and received and it is, therefore, vitally important for it to have a separate regulating body equipped to deal with the particular issues relevant to it. Moreover, because of the way in which radio and TV stations are licensed, broadcasters have always had a closer tie to statutory regulation. By contrast, the press – in its role as watchdog of those in power – has been free of governmental restrictions.*

This illustrates two essential differences between print and broadcast media that have been relied on to justify the different regulatory regimes. First, the active selection and purchase of newspapers (by contrast to the traditional view of passive broadcasting consumption), and secondly, the freedom to publish in print (by contrast to the licensing of broadcasting). However, both these assumptions must be revisited. On the broadcasting side, the selection of audiovisual material is increasingly active (through an extensive menu of channels on the electronic programme guide rather than a limited dial, often including options to pay for content) and the value of spectrum that has traditionally underpinned licensing is falling away (with digital switchover). On the print media side, many newspapers have not elected to place their electronic offerings behind a pay wall and these are generally freely available online without requiring an active purchase from the consumer. Whether material is being 'pushed' at or 'pulled' by the consumer is an increasingly obsolete notion.

While the role as 'watchdog of those in power' and safeguarding freedom of expression is central to the democratic value of the press, it is the issue of privacy, and the intrusion of the press, that underpins most clauses in the Editors' Code. The Editors' Code has specific clauses on accuracy, discrimination, financial journalism, confidential sources, and payments to witnesses and criminals. But the remaining clauses of the Editors' Code deal with issues of privacy and intrusion: respect for a 'private and family

45

life'; prohibitions on 'intimidation, harassment or persistent pursuit'; sensitivity required 'in cases involving personal grief or shock' and the reporting of suicide; interviewing or photographing of children, in particular while at school; identifying children and others in relation to crime including sexual offences; sensitive locations such as hospitals. In addition, clause 10, introduced in 2004, extended in 2007, and of particular interest to the 'Hackgate' allegations of 2011, states that:

> The press must not seek to obtain or publish material acquired by using hidden cameras or clandestine listening devices; or by intercepting private or mobile telephone calls, messages or emails; or by the unauthorised removal of documents or photographs; or by accessing digitally-held private information without consent.

Although the starting point is that such practices 'must not' be used, many clauses, including clause 10, are marked with an asterisk denoting that there may be exceptions if they 'can be demonstrated to be in the public interest', for example in 'detecting or exposing crime or serious impropriety' or 'preventing the public from being misled by an action or statement of an individual or organisation'. The Editors' Code also adds 'There is a public interest in freedom of expression itself'.

But while the Editors' Code says it is designed to safeguard freedom of expression, the PCC accepts that this is not a concept that can be taken for granted in the public's consciousness. In 2010 the PCC conducted small-scale qualitative research among four focus groups for internal purposes, in order to inform its understanding of public attitudes. Stephen Abell, the PCC's Director, concluded from observing the focus groups that:

> People have a very vague sense of freedom of expression and therefore they read the papers and they expect them to be partial, but they don't necessarily link partiality with freedom of expression very easily ... when you live in a country where freedom of expression has been established so strongly as in this country, I think it is very much to the back of people's minds. It doesn't seem to me to be a pressing notion to them. When we did these focus groups they were led though discussions. By the end of it, when they had thought about all the balancing of rights and freedom of expression, privacy and the right for the public to know, and the right for editors to make editorial decisions, they came to the conclusion that, yes, partiality – the ability to say what you think – is really important. But it wasn't something that was intrinsic to them when they sat down, which I found to be really interesting. The lesson we took from that is that if part of the existence of the PCC protects freedom of expression, allows newspapers to contain partial comment, which I believe is of benefit to a democratic society, it does need to be an argument made to people rather than an automatic assumption.[84]

Just as privacy and intrusion are central to the standards set out in the Editors' Code, so too they have underpinned changes to the Code, and to the PCC itself, since their inception and will be pertinent to the deliberations of the Leveson Inquiry.

[84] Interview May 2011.

4.2. The survival of press self-regulation

The PCC fiercely prizes self-regulation as a corner stone of the promotion of press freedom. In particular it supports its members' resistance to any notion of licensing the press.[85]

The origins of the PCC lie with the Royal Commission on the Press under Sir William Ross which in 1949 recommended a general council of the press 'to safeguard liberties and rebuke excesses'.[86] The Press Council was created in 1953 'to maintain high ethical standards of journalism and to promote press freedom' and combined the roles of defender of freedoms and adjudicator on complaints. By 1977 the Report of the Royal Commission on the Press concluded that the Press Council was failing to regulate the press industry. In the 1980s concerns about the efficacy of the Press Council, and in particular concerns about infringements of privacy and right of reply led to more urgent calls for statutory regulation. David Calcutt was appointed, with a remit that would not have looked out of place in the terms of reference of the Leveson Inquiry:

> to consider what measures (whether legislative or otherwise) are needed to give further protection to individual privacy from the activities of the press and improve recourse against the press for the individual citizen.[87]

His conclusion in the 1990 Calcutt report was to recommend replacing the Press Council with a new Press Complaints Commission, with the threat of statutory regulation should it fail to raise and maintain standards. The PCC had 18 months to demonstrate 'that non-statutory self-regulation can be made to work effectively' and was left in no doubt by Calcutt that 'This is a stiff test for the press. If it fails, we recommend that a statutory system for handling complaints should be introduced.'

The PCC was established in 1991 and introduced the first 16-clause Code of Practice. While the PCC is charged with administering and enforcing the Editors' Code of Practice, the Code itself is drawn up by a committee of editors. Within two years Calcutt concluded that it was failing and that his original proposals (for statutory regulation) should be implemented. He proposed a 'Statutory Tribunal' with powers to enforce publication of its adjudications, impose fines, and award compensation, with jurisdiction over 'the publishers of all newspapers ... and all magazines ... which are published commercially'. In addition, his report *Review of Press Self-Regulation* recommended the consideration of legislation in relation to privacy and the interception of telecommunications.[88]

Instead, however, the response was to tighten the Editors' Code, in particular in relation to 'clandestine listening devices', and this was further tightened following the death of Diana, Princess of Wales, in 1997 when the words 'should not' were replaced with 'must not' throughout.[89]

In 2003 the House of Commons Culture, Media and Sport Committee published its report *Privacy and Media Intrusion*[90] and, following a range of oral and written evidence, reflected on the differing regulatory regimes for broadcasting and the press:

---

[85] The Licensing of the Press Act of 1662, 'An Act for preventing the frequent Abuses in printing seditious treasonable and unlicensed Bookes and Pamphlets and for regulating of Printing and Printing Presses' (http://www.british-history.ac.uk/re-port.aspx?compid=47336), was repealed in 1863. Since then the press has been free of statutory regulation.
[86] http://www.publications.parliament.uk/pa/cm200203/cmselect/cmcumeds/458/458.pdf.
[87] D. Calcutt et al., *Report of the Committee on Privacy and Related Matters*, Chairman David Calcutt QC (London: HMSO, 1990; Cm. 1102), n. 1, para 1.1.
[88] http://www.official-documents.gov.uk/document/cm21/2135/2135.pdf.
[89] In addition in 1997 PCC and the Code were made applicable to online versions of publications and audio-visual material that appears on a publication's website discussed below.
[90] http://www.publications.parliament.uk/pa/cm200203/cmselect/cmcumeds/458/458.pdf.

The broadcasters and the press operated in two quite different environments. The broadcasters, being near-monopoly providers delivering output straight into people's homes, were licensed, regulated by statute – including a requirement for impartial news provision – and subject, ultimately, to the removal of their licence to operate if they continually transgressed. The BBC was of course in a slightly different position constitutionally, but the implications of the Royal Charter and Agreement with the Secretary of State were effectively the same. The press was in a different position. As Mr Paul Dacre, editor of The Daily Mail, told us: 'anyone can start a newspaper'. In the absence of a wholly new statutory system, there was ultimately no big stick, or Damoclean sword, under which change could be imposed. Therefore, the current regulation of the press is a matter of consensus and voluntary submission ... Mr James Strachan, barrister, pointed to the anomaly of proposals to give the PCC 'teeth' because this, he argued, misunderstands the basic position that 'any coercive means the regulator wishes to impose have to be by the consent of those ... being regulated'.

The Committee was tasked with balancing a democratic society's 'resolute guarantee of freedom of speech, especially for the media' with 'respect for privacy'. It commented:

The balancing of these rights, or their due reconciliation, is what this Report is about. In 1993, with regard to the press, the balance being struck was not found to be appropriate by the Review of Press Self-Regulation carried out by Sir David Calcutt QC, nor, subsequently, by our predecessor Committee [the National Heritage Committee's 1993 inquiry].

Subsequent Select Committees have continued to find that the balance between guaranteeing freedom of speech and respecting privacy has not been appropriately struck with regard to the press. But, in the absence of a 'big stick or Damoclean sword', Select Committees continued to support self-regulation. Their 2007 publication *Self-Regulation and the Press*[91] and the 2010 publication *Press Standards, Privacy and Libel*[92] criticised the PCC for inactivity over particular coverage. The 2007 Select Committee concentrated on the media scrum that attended Kate Middleton on her twenty-fifth birthday; the 2010 report considered the successful prosecution of the *News of the World* by Max Mosley for breach of privacy and the coverage of the disappearance of Madeleine McCann. However, so rapidly did concerns over new stories keep arising, that each time the Committee tried to draw the inquiry to a close 'fresh developments occurred which warranted examination and inclusion', including successive phone-hacking allegations.

The 2010 report pulled no punches in a concluding paragraph, which it highlighted in bold, condemning 'without reservation' a culture 'in the newsroom of *The News of the World* and other newspapers at the time which at best turned a blind eye to illegal activities such as phone-hacking and blagging[93] and at worst actively condoned it' and expressed the belief that it had done substantial damage to the newspaper industry as a whole:

---

[91] http://www.parliament.the-stationery-office.co.uk/pa/cm200607/cmselect/cmcumeds/375/375.pdf.
[92] http://www.publications.parliament.uk/pa/cm200910/cmselect/cmcumeds/362/36202.htm.
[93] House of Commons Home Affairs Committee report on 'Unauthorised tapping into or hacking of mobile communications' of July 2011 explains that: '"Blagging" is where an unauthorised person obtains personal information – addresses, telephone numbers, medical information, financial information, etc – from a source that legitimately hold the information by pretending to be either the individual whose information is held or someone else with a legitimate right to access the information.' http://www.parliament.uk/documents/commons-committees/home-affairs/unauthorised_tapping_or_hacking_mobile_communications_report.pdf.

We have repeatedly encountered an unwillingness to provide the detailed information that we sought, claims of ignorance or lack of recall, and deliberate obfuscation. We strongly condemn this behaviour which reinforces the widely held impression that the press generally regard themselves as unaccountable.

However, having vented its spleen about the most recent scandal to have surfaced, and having suggested the strengthening of the Editors' Code (the 2010 Committee described it as 'toothless' and noted that the PCC neither had, nor sought, the power to impose fines and was often bypassed in favour of people seeking redress through the courts), each Select Committee has ultimately endorsed the current self-regulatory model. The 2010 Committee proposed that the PCC should be able to impose a financial penalty and in the most serious of cases 'the suspension of printing of the offending publication for one issue'. However, in relation to the principle of self- or statutory regulation, it concluded that 'self-regulation of the press is greatly preferable to statutory regulation, and should continue'.

The PCC, in a March 2010 response to the Select Committee's report, said it 'believes its powers are effective'. It said it would talk to the industry about the issue of sanctions but continued:

The Commission does want to take this opportunity seriously to question whether the suspension of printing of an offending publication – even if that were practicable – could ever be proportionate and appropriate in a democratic society. As far as the Commission can determine, no other analogous body in the civilised world would employ such a sanction.

Indeed back in 1993 Calcutt, even while he proposed immediate introduction of statutory regulation of the press, had balked at the idea of such a sanction. He had observed:

It is one thing to prevent the press from publishing material which is in contravention of the code; it is quite another to prevent it from publishing legitimate information because of earlier breaches. In my view this would amount to censorship of an unacceptable kind.[94]

In July 2010 the PCC published its Governance Review[95] which endorsed some elements of the Select Committee's recommendations, and the recommendations of the Media Standards Trust,[96] for example, setting out that there should be greater proactivity in investigating areas of concern, rather than awaiting complaints, and a more prominent role for the lay members of the PCC Board including representation of the 'lay voice' in reviews of the Code. It noted that the ratio of 10 lay members on the Commission to 7 editors had increased since 1991 and was higher than the ratio to be found in other European press councils.[97]

The Review referred to the stinging criticism of the PCC as 'toothless' and said that the 'ladder of sanctions' available to the PCC from publication of a critical adjudication through to referral by the PCC of the editor to the publisher for disciplinary action should be spelled out clearly. Nevertheless, it concluded: 'the introduction of fines would not benefit the system (they could be budgeted for by major publications, but could cripple

---

[94] http://www.official-documents.gov.uk/document/cm21/2135/2135.pdf.
[95] http://www.pcc.org.uk/assets/441/Independent_Governance_Review_Report.pdf.
[96] http://mediastandardstrust.org/wp-content/uploads/downloads/2010/08/Reforming-independent-self-regulation.pdf.
[97] Ian Barber and Lewis Evans, 'Review of the New Zealand Press Council' (2007), available at
http://www.presscouncil.org.nz/articles/press_council_review.pdf.

smaller titles; they would introduce confrontation into a collaborative approach that generally works well)'.

The issue of introducing fines, and other sanctions with 'teeth', went to the heart of the self-regulatory conundrum acknowledged by the 2003 Committee above, namely that coercion sits uncomfortably in a consensual framework of self-regulation. Nor, argued Eve Salomon, former PCC Commissioner, are fines in tune with consumer attitudes. She pointed to PCC research that found three-quarters of respondents preferred a prompt public apology to a fine:

> I know certain detractors say the PCC is ineffective because it doesn't fine. We've done research on this,[98] consumers aren't looking for a power to fine. The real sanction, and the one that Editors avoid more than anything, is having an adjudication made against them.[99]

Hitherto, tightening the Editors' Code has kept successive Select Committees at bay, though as discussed above at the time of writing the future of self-regulation for the press and issues of privacy are subject to the considerations of the Leveson Inquiry and of a joint committee of Parliament charged with examining the law in relation to privacy injunctions.[100] However, other factors have also surfaced in recent years that have challenged the PCC's ability properly to regulate the press.

The preamble to the Editors' Code asserts that with rights come responsibilities; the right of freedom of expression, together with the potential for influence over hearts and minds, is matched by ethical responsibilities. Accordingly, the preamble to the Code[101] states that:

> All members of the press have a duty to maintain the highest professional standards. The Code, which includes this preamble and the public interest exceptions below, sets the benchmark for those ethical standards, protecting both the rights of the individual and the public's right to know.

It goes on to observe that the Code 'is the cornerstone of the system of self-regulation to which the industry has made a binding commitment'.

There are two significant challenges to these claims. First, as discussed above, the phone-hacking scandal has exposed stark gaps in the 'binding commitment' of some members to basic, let alone onerous, ethical standards. Secondly, the PCC's claim to represent 'the industry' has been undermined in recent years.

Notable in this regard have been *Guardian* editor Alan Rusbridger's resignation from the Editors' Code Committee in 2009 over the ineffectiveness of the PCC's inquiry into the *News of the World* phone-hacking allegations,[102] and the withdrawal from the PCC's jurisdiction of Richard Desmond's Northern and Shell titles (including the *Daily Express, Sunday Express, Daily Star, Daily Star Sunday,* and *OK!* magazine) following the non-payment of fees in 2011.[103] In relation to the latter, Professor Roy Greenslade argued at the time that MPs may use the withdrawal of these national newspapers 'as a way of reopening the debate about statutory regulation' and noted that:

---

[98] PCC/Toluna public attitudes survey 2010: http://www.pcc.org.uk/assets/111/PCC_Survey_2010.pdf.
[99] Interview May 2011.
[100] http://services.parliament.uk/hansard/Commons/bydate/20110523/mainchamberdebates/part003.html.
[101] http://www.pcc.org.uk/cop/practice.html.
[102] *PCC Report on Phone Message Tapping Allegations,* publ. 9 Nov. 2009 and withdrawn 6 July 2011: http://www.pcc.org.uk/news/index.html?article=NjAyOA==.
[103] http://www.pcc.org.uk/news/index.html?article=Njg3NA==.

John Whittingdale, chairman of the Commons Culture, Media and Sport Select Committee, said: 'I regard the exclusion as a very serious development. The committee is on record as saying that if self-regulation is to have any credibility it must encompass all the major publishers. This now creates doubt about its efficacy.'[104]

Stephen Abell of the PCC argued, in an interview prior to the phone-hacking revelations of July 2011, that there is a constant drive to raise standards but saw a certain inevitability to the 'never-ending' challenge and criticism levelled at the PCC. Its membership is voluntary, not subject to statutory compulsion, and publishers therefore make choices over membership. While self-regulation, and the lack of a statutory basis, is a corner stone on which the PCC argue freedom of speech is safeguarded, with it, Abell observed, comes the need to constantly justify the PCC's existence:

If you are Ofcom you have a statutory underpinning, you have a guaranteed – although governments come in and trim it – role here. The PCC is based on co-operation and good will. So if you work at the PCC almost every day you have to work to justify it. Every time a call comes in at 11 o'clock at night with someone with a problem, you don't want that case to be the case that raises a question about the PCC. You have to make it work.[105]

And there is a further challenge to making the current regulatory system work. Newspapers are now competing in online markets, indeed, the *Guardian*'s future has recently been positioned as online rather than print in a 'digital first' strategy. Editor Alan Rusbridger explained to the BBC's *Media Show:*[106]

I think print is essentially already a broken economic model. This idea of expensive printing sites, vans trundling throughout the night, wholesalers, news agents, paper boys - I mean it's a Victorian chain of distribution and I don't think there's much comfort for the print nostalgists in that model going forward.

However, in the shorter term he pointed to complementary roles for the printed and online *Guardian* content, not as paper and digital versions of the same newspaper, but as complementary offerings of comment and news respectively:

We've done a lot of research about how people are consuming the Guardian in all forms now. People who are the loyalists in print – 50% of them are reading it in the evening and only 4% say 'we actually turn to it for breaking news to learn new things'. And I think those are two highly significant figures … I think we can do a paper that does a better job of – not telling people what has happened, you can do that on the web – but helping them to make sense of it … that doesn't mean we are bailing out of news in the whole universe of what the Guardian does … we'll do as much news on the web, but the paper will have a different kind of feel.

---

[104] http://www.guardian.co.uk/media/greenslade/2011/jan/11/richard-desmond-houseofcommons.
[105] Interview May 2011.
[106] http://www.bbc.co.uk/iplayer/episode/b011zn6b/The_Media_Show_22_06_2011.

Future regulation of newspapers requires the flexibility to respond to new offerings delivered in print and online through a range of devices and, as discussed below, this has been recognised by the PCC in recent years.

4.3. Online newspapers compete in the unregulated world of the internet

Since 1997 the PCC's remit has been widened to include editorial content on publications' websites and in 2007 this was extended to include audiovisual material appearing on newspaper and magazine websites. In addition, from December 2009, the PCC's remit included online-only publications. The PCC's philosophy in relation to online content has been to link regulation to a positive differentiation from unregulated journalism and, as we shall see in Chapter 6, to accreditation. In Stephen Abell's view:

> *Standards should be a selling point for news providers, particularly online. I think it's of real benefit to the press here that if a gossip goes around about something, you're probably not going to believe it until you see it in regulated content. When Michael Jackson died TMZ broke the blog.[107] Then there were huge surges on other mainstream media news sites to see if it was true ... If you want to have intrusive gossipy content then regulation will push you away from that, but if it's stuff where you want to know if it's true, if it's been properly investigated, properly checked, there's a degree of proper journalism that can be tested and challenged, then there is an advantage to mainstream media.[108]*

To this end the PCC has encouraged the titles that sign up to its regulation to make their membership clear to consumers, within the printed newspapers (for example, on letters pages) and on online pages.

In 2007 the PCC noted that for the first time it received more complaints about online versions of articles (56%) than hard-copy versions (44%). However it observed:

> *Since February 2007, the PCC has only received a handful of complaints about audio-visual material ... they generally conform to a particular pattern: they relate to the area of privacy; and they comprise video taken and submitted by non-journalists, which is employed to illustrate stories about individuals' conduct.[109]*

The following case study is typical of this pattern, and illustrates how the PCC has extended the use of the Editors' Code, and in this case the tests applied to privacy, to apply to embedded online newspaper content.

PCC case study: the *Hamilton Advertiser*

The first upheld complaint in relation to online content was made by Mrs Laura Gaddis, PTA president at John Ogilvie High School, who complained about an article published in the *Hamilton Advertiser* in 2007.[110] The article reported that a 16-year-old had filmed her unruly maths class at school on her mobile phone in order to explain poor results to her parents. Still images from the video were published in the newspaper and moving

---

[107] http://www.tmz.com/2009/06/25/michael-jackson-rushed-to-the-hospital.
[108] Interview May 2011.
[109] http://www.pcc.org.uk/news/newsletter/april/online.html.
[110] http://www.pcc.org.uk/cases/adjudicated.html?article=NDY2MA==.

images were published on its website. The complainant said no permission had been given for filming and no contact made with the school to determine whether this was a genuine problem or one-off incident.

The newspaper argued there was a clear public interest in the lack of supervision demonstrated by the video, and the footage did not intrude into the education of the children featured, all of whom were over 16. However, it said it had removed the video from its website. It also argued that to have obscured the faces of the pupils in the stills would have undermined the impact of the story.

The PCC found that, while the story was clearly one of considerable public interest, this did not override the pupils' rights under the Code. It said either steps should have been taken to conceal their identity, or proper consent should have been obtained: 'Not doing so amounted to an unnecessary intrusion into the pupils' time at school in breach of Clause 6'.

The basic tests underlying this PCC adjudication are very similar to those Ofcom applies. A complaint to Ofcom from the mother of a girl filmed for a Channel 4 *Dispatches* programme, also published in 2007,[111] followed a very similar argument. The girl was filmed by an undercover teacher recording an unruly class. Ofcom considered that the girl's privacy had been infringed in both the making and broadcast of the programme but that this was warranted by the public interest in the subject matter and significantly in this case, as opposed to the PCC example, the broadcaster had taken responsible steps to conceal her identity. While the PCC published a brief summary of its decision (to uphold), and Ofcom detailed its decision (not to uphold) in 15 pages, the nub of the issues was the same for both bodies: was there an infringement of privacy and if so was it justified?

Philosophically, Abell argued, the PCC is very close to Ofcom in the approach it takes to regulating audiovisual material, as illustrated in the above consistency with which both bodies apply rules on privacy in relation to sensitive locations such as schools.

In addition, Abell argued that much of the audiovisual material included on newspaper websites is 'pre-regulated' in the sense that it has already been broadcast and therefore subject to Ofcom's requirements. By way of example he noted that the *Daily Mail* uses ITN content online. Embedded audiovisual material is not, he said, generating many complaints and he attributed this to the nature of the audiovisual content on newspaper websites:

> Most newspapers' [audio visual] content is still very subordinate to the written word. It's illustrative material, content that would have been taken as stills in the paper. So lots of the content is still directly analogous to what would have gone in the paper. Clause 5 [of the Editors' Code] deals with grief and shock and we sometimes get complaints about moving pictures around death scenes, but the Code is able to deal with that relatively easily ... very rarely have people written to say this audiovisual content is offensive or tasteless.[112]

The Editors' Code may not have specific clauses in relation to harm and offence but essentially the market, reflected in consumer expectations of particular brands, appears to be determining editors' choices, just as it has traditionally done in print. In this way Abell argued that newspaper editors are bringing the same editorial decision-making to potentially harmful or offensive audiovisual material that they have always brought to

---

[111] http://stakeholders.ofcom.org.uk/binaries/enforcement/broadcast-bulletins/obb77/issue77.pdf.
[112] Interview May 2011.

dealing with potentially shocking front-page photographs or war coverage: 'They [Editors] have a sense of what their readers expect in terms of taste and decency. The *Daily Mail*, for example, has a sense of what *Daily Mail* readers would like to see, the *Guardian* the same.' In addition Abell argued that the experience of consuming online newspaper content is active, by contrast to the traditional view of viewing and listening:

> It [online newspaper audiovisual material] is not being broadcast to passive consumption: you go onto the Guardian or Daily Mail website, you click on the article, you read the story and look at the footage linked to it as you would pictures. Now that may change as you move to a model where you have internet-connected television but even then that active selection and consumption, in the context of a news story, will remain.[113]

And yet the power of broadcast audiovisual material to influence hearts and minds has informed the public protection requirements that underpin the statutory impartiality and harm and offence rules in the Ofcom Code. With no such rules in the Editors' Code there is considerable potential for confusion, particularly when online newspaper audiovisual content is available through an internet-connected television, and is therefore increasingly difficult to distinguish from content that is being broadcast.

The above example of the relationship between the *Daily Mail* and ITN raises a number of pertinent questions. How far is the regulation of ITN material on the *Daily Mail* online site clear? Does the consumer readily understand who has editorial responsibility for the material, and who will deal with complaints about it? Should consumers expect the material to be impartial (as required of ITN material if broadcast, but not required of print or online newspaper content under the PCC Code)? Does ITN maintain editorial control over the material? If the material has been found in breach of the Ofcom Code would it still be permitted to be shown on the newspaper website? If the material would be subject to scheduling restrictions (for example, the 9pm watershed) when broadcast, is this apparent to parents and children? These are issues to which Chapters 7 and 10 return.

As online publication becomes increasingly important to newspaper revenues, Martin Moore of the Media Standards Trust foresaw further tensions as different ends of the newspaper industry compete in different ways in online markets. In Moore's view the PCC's regulatory framework worked in the past because:

> It was quite a comprehensive system based on a very identifiable medium which was paper and so you could work out who was part of the system and who wasn't very easily, because if it was on paper it was part of the PCC and if it wasn't it wasn't. And equally it bestraddled two sides: on the one hand it was a lowest common denominator saying 'you can't fall below these standards', at the same time it was saying 'we're trying to encourage high standards and help people aspire to high standards'.

However, before the 2011 phone-hacking scandal fully erupted, he identified 'big tensions inherent with it':

> The reason I think it's so difficult to sustain that, and there are so many tensions inherent, is that it's no longer comprehensive. Express Newspapers have pulled out, and there will be quite a lot of incentives for those at the lower end of the market to pull out because they're thinking, 'hang on a

---

[113] Interview May 2011.

> *second, I'm competing with everyone on the internet, all the people who are*
> *outside these constraints – I'm constraining myself unnecessarily'. So it will*
> *be quite tempting for others to drop out from the bottom end. At the top end*
> *many of those will be thinking: 'we compete at an international level*
> *particularly online and in digital media ... why are we part of this system?'[114]*

Moore appeared to be identifying a shift in the regulatory centre of gravity for newspapers. Traditionally, newspaper self-regulation has been justified against a backdrop of statutory regulation for television and radio. Yet online newspapers are competing, as Moore pointed out, against the backdrop of the unregulated world of the internet. While the PCC has sought to promote its membership as a selling-point linked to standards, Moore observed:

> *Our impression is specifically those at the higher end of the market don't*
> *advertise the fact that they're part of the PCC, particularly because they don't*
> *think it adds especially to people's trust in them. And in the future that seems*
> *to me to be quite a significant problem, because if one of the big reasons for*
> *being part of a self regulatory system is aspirational then if you don't think*
> *it adds to your brand why on earth are you in it?*

One answer to Moore's question is that the members of the PCC are not bound together by common ethical standards so much as by a common interest in seeing off statutory regulatory interventions. In any event, in addition to the tensions between the up- and down-market ends of the PCC membership spectrum, and how far either end is incentivised to remain a member in an online media world, there is another area with which press regulation must struggle. This relates to responsibility for certain audiovisual media content, hitherto regulated by the PCC, being claimed by a new body, the Authority for Television on Demand, and is discussed in Chapter 5 below.

4.4. Proposal for independent, voluntary, incentivised, transparent press regulation: recognised in statute and robust in its requirements

While it is not the purpose here to set out all the competing alternatives for the future regulation of the press, it is worth noting that, although immediate responses to the phone-hacking scandal have again surfaced the possibility of statutory press regulation, these have been modulated from within and without the industry by calls for 'independent' regulation or a 'professional body' with robust regulatory and disciplinary authority.[115]

The question at the heart of such debate is whether regulation of the press will continue to be voluntary and if so how it will retain credibility if it does not embrace all newspaper and magazine titles. Current regulation by the PCC has been roundly condemned not just from outside, but also by newspaper editors themselves,[116] nor can consumers identify in a meaningful way those titles that have withdrawn from its jurisdiction.

---

[114] Interview May 2011.
[115] The views of a number of newspaper editors are represented in:
http://www.pressgazette.co.uk/story.asp?sectioncode=1&storycode=47710&c=1 and http://www.ft.com/cms/s/0/354ad55c-e3b5-11e0-bd3d-00144feabdc0.html#axzz1YaZQLDob.
[116] http://www.pressgazette.co.uk/story.asp?sectioncode=1&storycode=47877&c=1.

It is the contention of this report that informed choice for consumers and incentivised choice for providers is the key to these regulatory dilemmas: choice exercised by consumers over engagement with regulated and unregulated content, and supported by transparent messaging. Choice exercised by the press and other new media providers over whether adherence to voluntary standards, for example on privacy, separation of fact and opinion, accuracy in news, a right of reply and ethical conduct, is commercially and ethically valuable.

In this way the press would retain the freedoms and privileges on which its journalism is founded (referred to below) but would also have a voluntary but clear mechanism for acknowledging the duties and responsibilities that accompany them. It would be incentivised to adhere to robustly enforced standards, as a demonstration of those commitments in print and online, and consumers would be provided with clarity over whether individual titles choose to operate within the regulated or unregulated public space.

The following key principles are proposed to underpin such a model of press regulation:

- Independence: the proposed model would be independent, of both the industry and the state, in its administration and enforcement of regulatory requirements. It would be funded, and its rules established, by industry, but the independence of its decision-making and robustness of its sanctions would be guaranteed, for example, through the composition of its chairman and board members and by procedures for dealing with complaints and investigations.
- Statutory recognition: while the proposed model of regulation would be entirely independent of government and the state, it would be provided with recognition in statute. This would lay a secure foundation for its authority and independence, including the composition of its board, and a recognition of a range of procedures and sanctions. It would not confer statutory powers since the basis for its authority would be voluntary membership, but would provide a link to a number of privileges associated with membership (discussed below).
- Transparency: this core requirement would enable the consumer to make informed choices about consumption of newspapers and other journalism, whether via print or online. Essentially the consumer would be able to discriminate between the regulated and the unregulated, between those who have made a commitment to regulatory requirements and those who have rejected such a commitment. Transparency would be achieved through an associated standards mark clearly flagged in print and online.
- Incentivised voluntary participation: newspapers and wider journalists, including independent bloggers, would have the choice of using standards as a selling point and enjoying associated benefits, or operating outside the regulated sphere and simply within the minimum requirements of the law, as is the case for unregulated online content. Benefits and privileges attached to such membership would require detailed consideration but could build on public recognition of regulatory participation:

  - recognition by the courts in relation to privacy cases[117] and related penalties; also in relation to libel cases where the courts recognise, for example, journalists' particular rights to freedom of expression 'subject to the proviso that they act in good faith in order to provide accurate and reliable

---

[117] At the time of writing Joint Committee consideration is being given to privacy and superinjunctions: http://services.parliament.uk/hansard/Commons/bydate/20110523/mainchamberdebates/part003.html.

information in accordance with responsible journalism'.[118] Adherence to this model of voluntary, independent regulation would provide a demonstration of values, accountability, and association with 'responsible journalism';

- the ability to attract favourable advertising and search engine associations based on content credibility;
- the benefits of accreditation in relation to court reporting and access to government and other information (discussed further below in Chapter 6);
- potential taxation and charitable incentives as considered in the Reuters Institute for the Study of Journalism publication *What's Happening to our News*[119] which proposed extending and strengthening tax concessions and reviewing charitable status in relation to the civic value and public benefit of journalism;
- association with other regulated media and the ability to differentiate regulated newspaper and other journalistic offerings from confusion with unregulated content whether in print or online.

- Credible investigations and sanctions: in return for the benefits of membership, the regulated press would be required to agree and accept a range of sanctions and investigatory procedures at the disposal of the new regulatory body, including suspension and expulsion from its membership and associated benefits.

In this way the freedoms of the press would be supported, and its accountability ensured. Those operating outside its framework would do so transparently, excluded from the privileges of responsible journalism, but (as with any currently unregulated provider) within the scope of the law.

One example where the model of a voluntary, yet statutorily recognised, press regulator has been established is Ireland.

Ireland: independent, voluntary press regulation recognised in statute

Ireland offers an example of press regulation connected to statute without compelling membership. Set up in 2008 the Press Council of Ireland's objectives are very similar to those of the PCC:

> to provide the public with an independent forum for resolving complaints about the press; to resolve all complaints quickly, fairly and free of charge; and to defend the freedom of the press and the freedom of the public to be informed.[120]

It is independent of government and, while there are industry members on the Council, it says it is 'in operation, independent of the media' but operating 'with the co-operation of newspaper and magazine editors'. The Office of the Press Ombudsman deals with complaints in the first instance but can refer cases to the Press Council which also deals with appeals. Membership of the Press Council is voluntary and its work is paid for by a levy on members.

---

[118] European Court of Human Rights: Times Newspapers Ltd (No 1 and 2) v UK (n 23) [42], discussed further in Richard Danbury's legal research thesis 'Special Treatment of Institutional Journalistic Speech in English Law': http://ora.ouls.ox.ac.uk/objects/uuid%3A9360d896-c5b5-4607-a340-feb0757a3ca5/datastreams/THESIS01.

[119] http://reutersinstitute.politics.ox.ac.uk/fileadmin/documents/Publications/What_s_Happening_to_Our_News.pdf.

[120] http://www.presscouncil.ie/about-the-press-council.77.html.

Where the Irish Press Council really departs from the PCC model is the link to legislation. Ireland's Defamation Act 2009[121] explicitly recognises a body called the Press Council and offers substantial benefits, and therefore incentives, to members. Essentially the Act gives the regulatory structure a statutory footing and the courts take membership of the Council, and adherence to its Code, into account in defamation proceedings. The 2009 Annual Report of the Press Council of Ireland and Office of the Press Ombudsman explained:

> A key provision of the new Act, where the Press Council and Press Ombudsman are concerned, is that it facilitates and encourages publications, where appropriate, to apologise for errors without a potentially costly admission of legal liability. The recognition of the Press Council and the Press Ombudsman under the Act strengthens the role of the Office of the Press Ombudsman in negotiating satisfactory resolutions to complaints that may involve apologies where these are agreed and appropriate.
>
> Although it is technically possible for publications that are not member publications of the Press Council to claim similar privileges, they will have the difficult task, if they are to do so, of convincing a court that their standards and structures of accountability are no less rigorous and professional than those moderated by the Press Council. In these circumstances, membership of the Press Council will be, for all publications that have yet to take this step, a valuable asset.

Irish legislation sets out the principal objectives of the Press Council to: ensure the protection of freedom of expression of the press; protect the public interest by ensuring ethical, accurate and truthful reporting by the press; maintain certain minimum ethical and professional standards among the press; and ensure that the privacy and dignity of the individual is protected. It sets out requirements for its independence, the composition of its directors (equivalent to PCC Commissioners), its funding and investigations and hearings; and its powers to require the publication of a determination in any form and manner it directs.

Unlike statutory regulation under Ofcom, or co-regulation under ATVOD to be discussed in Chapter 5, membership of the Irish Press Council is voluntary. No system of licences (as in the case of Ofcom) nor notification (as in the case of ATVOD) exists. It provides a regulated press without imposing that regulation on the whole industry, with all the difficulties of defining which organisations, or individuals, should fall within its scope, and which modes of publication (print or online).

Chapter 10 proposes arrangements introducing an independent regulator whose administration, sanctions, procedures, privileges for members, and transparency for consumers are recognised in statute. Initially established in relation to press regulation (in print and online) the proposal would be for eventual extension to wider media providers on a voluntary basis under a new regulatory settlement across platforms that recognises, and addresses, the challenge of converging content.

---

[121] http://www.irishstatutebook.ie/pdf/2009/en.act.2009.0031.pdf.

5. Video On Demand Regulation

5.1. Co-regulation applies to audiovisual content provided 'on demand'

ATVOD, the Authority for Television on Demand, is the new kid on the regulatory block, designated by Ofcom in 2010 to regulate editorial content provided on 'television-like on-demand programme services'.[122] After extensive lobbying by the UK government to limit EU regulation of the internet as far as possible, this is the area to which it extends. Under the Audiovisual Media Services Directive[123] video on demand services are subject to two basic editorial (non-commercial) content provisions set out in the Box.

Box 2. Extracts from the EU Audiovisual Media Services Directive applicable to on-demand audiovisual media services (non-commercial editorial provisions)

Article 6
Member States shall ensure by appropriate means that audiovisual media services provided by media service providers under their jurisdiction do not contain any incitement to hatred based on race, sex, religion or nationality.

Article 12
Member States shall take appropriate measures to ensure that on-demand audiovisual media services provided by media service providers under their jurisdiction which might seriously impair the physical, mental or moral development of minors are only made available in such a way as to ensure that minors will not normally hear or see such on-demand audio¬visual media services.

In a nutshell, these services must not provide material that incites hatred (on grounds of race, sex, religion, or nationality), nor unrestricted access to material that seriously impairs children (though whether even hard-core pornography meets this criterion is, as discussed below, a matter of debate by European regulators). There are no further editorial requirements on harm or offence, nor on fairness, privacy, nor impartiality.

As we shall see, the differences between the comprehensive requirements of the Ofcom Broadcasting Code and minimal requirements of the ATVOD Code have not been fully apparent to consumers, given video on demand provision of time-shifted or catch-up services featuring programming that has previously been broadcast (and therefore subject to Ofcom's Broadcasting Code). However, video on demand services

---

[122] As discussed above in Ch. 3 an 'on-demand' audiovisual media service (such as iPlayer or ITV Player) is: 'an audiovisual media service provided by a media service provider for the viewing of programmes at the moment chosen by the user and at his individual request on the basis of a catalogue of programmes selected by the media service provider'.
[123] http://eur-lex.europa.eu/LexUriServ/LexUriServ.do?uri=OJ:L:2010:095:0001:0024:EN:PDF.

can provide original content (including news, current affairs, and other forms of journalism) that has never been broadcast, and therefore has been subject to no prior regulation.

In addition, as the *Frankie Boyle* case study in this section reveals, content can breach the Ofcom Code but be permitted on video on demand services under the more minimal ATVOD rules. This was not the case for video on demand material prior to ATVOD's designation on 18 March 2010. Until then ATVOD was a self-regulatory body titled the *Association* for Television on Demand whose functions were very different to the *Authority* that has replaced it. Ofcom explained the Association's duties in 2007 as follows:

> *The Communications Act 2003 excluded video-on-demand services from Ofcom's statutory control, in the expectation that industry would take responsibility for oversight of such services. The VoD industry subsequently created a self-regulatory institution, the Association for TV on Demand (ATVOD), which oversees consumer protection issues in relation to VoD services ... In the event that a complaint was upheld by Ofcom, ATVOD members would be required by the ATVOD code not to offer on-demand access to the offending programme.[124]*

There is no longer a requirement to prohibit programmes in breach of the Ofcom Code from video on demand services. Indeed, the full ATVOD Code of Conduct, from its days as an Association, no longer exists. Instead, the new Authority's remit is to regulate solely in accordance with the amendments made to the Communications Act 2003 by the Audiovisual Media Services Regulations 2009 and 2010[125] which, as we shall see, provide only for minimal protections that are close to the provisions of laws on incitement to hatred and obscene publications.

The regulatory model here, unlike those for broadcasting (statutory regulation) and the press (self-regulation) discussed above, is co-regulation, and is provided for in the amendments made to the Communications Act 2003. Under these amendments Ofcom has designated ATVOD to carry out regulatory functions, but Ofcom retains legislative 'back stop' powers. These include the power to impose statutory sanctions on providers who contravene its rules,[126] which could include suspension of the service or a fine of up to 5% of the provider's revenue or £250,000 if that is greater. The philosophy behind co-regulation is to delegate statutory powers to a body that works in partnership with, though independently of, the industry.[127] ATVOD's board comprises a balance of independent and 'non-independent' members, and works in partnership with industry through the ATVOD Industry Forum, although it is 'independent from industry's commercial interests' and its 'top priority is to protect consumers'.[128] While the old Association had 'members', the new Authority regulates 'notified services'. Providers of video on demand services must give ATVOD notification of their intention to provide a service and comply with ATVOD regulation.

The Authority therefore has teeth that its self-regulatory predecessor lacked, but places few editorial demands on the services it regulates. It also provides, as ATVOD's Chief Executive, Pete Johnson, observed, a truly platform-neutral regulatory framework:

---

[124] http://www.parliament.the-stationery-office.co.uk/pa/cm200607/cmselect/cmcumeds/375/375we13.htm.
[125] Section 368 of the Communications Act (amended by AVMS Regulations):
http://www.legislation.gov.uk/uksi/2010/419/regulation/4/made.
[126] http://www.atvod.co.uk/uploads/files/ATVOD_Rules_and_Guidance_Ed1.1_Mar_2011.pdf.
[127] ATVOD's Chair Ruth Evans reflects on the co-regulatory approach in her submission to the Communications Review:
http://www.atvod.co.uk/uploads/files/ATVODResponse_to_Jeremy_Hunt.pdf.
[128] http://www.atvod.co.uk/about-ATVOD.

One of the very interesting things about these new regulations for VOD [video on demand] is that they are platform neutral. Historically media regulation has been in silos according to distribution technology and that's not the case in relation to VOD. Whether it's distributed over the mobile phone network, through satellite, through cable, or just through the internet, it's subject to exactly the same rules ... It's intended to recognise the dynamic nature of what's happening with television-like content, and to provide a framework to deal with that in terms of consumer protection.[129]

5.2. Only two editorial rules apply to video on demand content

Debate about the rules governing video on demand content has, as discussed below, so far centred on the protection of children from hard-core pornography. The contribution of video on demand content to the wider public space in which journalism sits has not been debated. I argue here, however, that there is a significant role for video on demand content in the shared public space. Indeed, no one listening to Eric Schmidt's 2011 Edinburgh Television Festival MacTaggart Lecture[130] could be in any doubt of Google's view that the future of media content is on demand. It is therefore worth exploring the rules applicable to video on demand content in more detail in order to identify where ATVOD sits on the regulatory spectrum, what is and is not expected of journalism provided on video on demand services, and the different approaches to regulation that underpin differences between the (minimal) rules in relation to video on demand and (comprehensive) rules in relation to broadcast content.

Of the 26 pages of ATVOD rules and guidance (most of which relate to notification procedures and compliance), one page contains the two substantive editorial content rules, derived from the AVMS Directive whose extracts are set out above (as well as two detailed rules on commercial content). Related guidance demonstrates how high the bar is set in relation to breaching either rule.

Rule 10 states that: 'An on-demand programme service must not contain any material likely to incite hatred based on race, sex, religion or nationality.' Accompanying guidance explains that '"Hatred" is a strong word':

It is neither the purpose nor the intention of [the Communications Act 2003, amended by the Audiovisual Media Services Regulations] to restrict legitimate freedom of speech by prohibiting or restricting discussion, criticism or expressions of antipathy, dislike, ridicule, insult or abuse for groups covered by this requirement. For example, it is permissible to express criticism, dislike or ridicule of a religious belief system or its practices or urge its adherents to cease practising or to express views which are sexist, insulting or offensive but which stop short of being likely to incite hatred.

The other editorial rule deals with hard-core pornography. Before considering its requirement it is worth briefly rehearsing the rules for broadcast television. In considering 'hard-core' pornographic material classified 'R18'[131] by the BBFC, or its

[129] Interview May 2010.

[130] http://www.guardian.co.uk/media/interactive/2011/aug/26/eric-schmidt-mactaggart-lecture-full-text.

[131] The BBFC explains that: 'Sex works are works whose primary purpose is sexual arousal or stimulation. Sex works containing only material which may be simulated are generally passed '18'. Sex works containing clear images of real sex, strong fetish material, sexually explicit animated images, or other very strong sexual images will be confined to the 'R18' category...The 'R18' category is a special and legally restricted classification primarily for explicit works of consenting sex or strong fetish material involving adults. Films may only be shown to adults in specially licensed cinemas, and video works may be supplied to adults only in licensed sex shops.' http://www.bbfc.co.uk/classification/guidelines/

equivalent, Ofcom's Statement on the first Broadcasting Code explained that it 'considered it appropriate to take a more precautionary approach to this very explicit sexual material, given our statutory duties'. Taking into account a range of factors, including research on the then effectiveness of PIN (personal identification number) protection, and 1999 BBFC research on the effects of pornography on vulnerable children, it concluded that:

> *Ofcom considers there is a significant risk, that at least a proportion of children would be able to access R18 material if it were to be broadcast under current security mechanisms. Given the strength of this material and the absence of evidence demonstrating that children could be effectively protected, Ofcom considers a prohibition of this material, in the current environment and for the time being, consistent with its objective to set standards to protect the under-eighteens.*[132]

The Broadcasting Code therefore contains a straight ban on R18 (or equivalent) material, and places mandatory access restrictions on 'soft-core' pornography.

In relation to video on demand content, ATVOD Rule 11 states that:

> *If an on-demand programme service contains material which might seriously impair the physical, mental or moral development of persons under the age of eighteen, the material must be made available in a manner which secures that such persons will not normally see or hear it.*

This rule raises a number of questions about the nature of the material caught by it and consistency with regulation for mainstream television. What constitutes material that 'might seriously impair' under-18s? Would 'hard-core' pornographic content classified 'R18' by the British Board of Film Classification (BBFC), or its equivalent, be caught by this rule and subject to a PIN or other protective mechanism? If not, could R18 material be provided on demand without any mandatory access restrictions? How is this reconciled with rules for scheduled linear television which ban R18 material outright, and place 'soft-core' pornographic content behind mandatory access restrictions?

The Government was sufficiently concerned by the issue of protecting children to ask Ofcom to 'consider whether the new Regulations (as now implemented in the amended Act) provide sufficient protection for children and young people with regard to sexually explicit content'.[133] Ofcom published its detailed report *Sexually Explicit Material and Video On Demand Services*[134] in August 2011 and recommended that the Government introduce new legislation for video on demand services which would specifically

> *prohibit R18 material from being included in UK-based VOD services unless appropriate mandatory restrictions are in place; and prohibit altogether from UK-based VOD services material whose content the BBFC would refuse to classify i.e. material stronger than R18.*

The Government has committed to considering these recommendations[135] and in the interim ATVOD Guidance advises that R18 material should be restricted for example by a PIN Code.[136]

[132] http://stakeholders.ofcom.org.uk/binaries/consultations/Broadcasting_code/statement/260994_new.pdf.

[133] http://www.atvod.co.uk/uploads/files/ATVOD_Rules_and_Guidance_Ed1.1_Mar_2011.pdf.

[134] http://stakeholders.ofcom.org.uk/binaries/internet/explicit-material-vod.pdf.

[135] http://www.culture.gov.uk/news/media_releases/8368.aspx.

[136] http://www.atvod.co.uk/uploads/files/ATVOD_Rules_and_Guidance_Ed1.1_Mar_2011.pdf.

Thus, in the case of scheduled, linear television, hard-core pornography is banned outright, and soft-core pornography is subject to mandatory access restrictions; whereas for video on demand services it is proposed that hard-core pornography would be subject to access restrictions, but on demand soft-core pornography would be subject to none.

The difference in approaches between video on demand and broadcast content reflects, or assumes, different contexts of the scheduled and on demand experiences. Scheduled, linear material is seen as pushed onto the consumer, while video on demand material is understood to be actively chosen. As discussed in Chapter 4 in relation to press regulation, the distinctions between the two blur in the blended experience of internet-connected television, and the justification for these different approaches begins to fall away.

The more selective approach to broadcast material through the electronic programme guide and enhanced PIN protections, could argue for a relaxation of scheduled, linear restrictions in the area of adult content and more widely. On the other hand, concerns about particular vulnerabilities and the adequacy of PINs could support a more precautionary approach to adult material on video on demand services. Chapter 9 returns to this in relation to the Bailey Review of child sexualisation[137] and so do the recommendations in Chapter 10. More significantly, in relation to journalism there is, as we shall see, an incoherence between the regulation of broadcast and video on demand content. As the two become increasingly indistinguishable, such incoherence threatens to undermine trust in each.

In addition to the two editorial rules are two detailed commercial rules. One is devoted to sponsorship and includes prohibitions on the promotion of tobacco products and prescription-only medicines; prohibitions on the sponsorship of news and current affairs; the preservation of editorial independence; and restrictions on alcohol sponsorship. The second contains similar prohibitions and restrictions in relation to product placement.

Given the limited editorial rules enforced by ATVOD, and the comprehensive rules imposed by Ofcom, it is perfectly possible for the same programme to breach Ofcom's Broadcasting Code as a scheduled, linear broadcast, but not breach ATVOD's rules when provided on demand. This is illustrated in the following case study.

ATVOD case study: Frankie Boyle's Tramadol Nights

ATVOD's first *Complaints Bulletin,* published 21 March 2011,[138] details its finding in relation to an episode of Channel 4's *Frankie Boyle's Tramadol Nights.* The adjudication reveals how high the bar is set in order for video on demand material to be found in breach.

It is instructive first to consider the Ofcom finding[139] in relation to the broadcast of the same episode on Channel 4 on 7 December 2010. Ofcom described *Tramadol Nights* as a six-part comedy series which was written by and featured the controversial, alternative comedian Frankie Boyle in various stand-up and comedy sketches which covered topics such as AIDS, cancer, religion, racism, sex, paedophilia, rape, incest, war, and disability. In the programme:

---

[137] https://www.education.gov.uk/publications/eOrderingDownload/Bailey%20Review.pdf.
[138] http://www.atvod.co.uk/uploads/files/Complaints_bulletin_no_1_210311.pdf.
[139] http://stakeholders.ofcom.org.uk/binaries/enforcement/broadcast-bulletins/obb179/obb179.pdf.

Frankie Boyle made various comments about the former glamour model and reality TV personality, Katie Price (formerly known as Jordan), and her eight year-old son, Harvey, who is known to have a medical condition and learning difficulties. Frankie Boyle said:

'Apparently Jordan and Peter Andre [Katie Price's ex-husband] are fighting each other over custody of Harvey. Well eventually one of them will have to lose and have to keep him. I have a theory that Jordan married a cage fighter [Alex Reid, Katie Price's second husband] because she needed someone strong enough to stop Harvey from fucking her.'

Katie Price's solicitors 'informed Ofcom that Harvey has a condition called septo-optic dysplasia, and is also on the autistic spectrum'. They stated that 'Harvey has very restricted sight, needs constant medication and has learning difficulties. Harvey, as a result of his condition and medication is large and strong for his age.'

Ofcom received 500 complaints and sought a response for Channel 4 in relation to whether generally accepted standards had been applied so as to provide adequate protection for members of the public from the inclusion of harmful and/or offensive material. The broadcaster acknowledged the 'undeniably difficult concepts this series contains'. It argued that 'the first part of the joke was aimed clearly at Katie Price and Peter Andre, painting them as cynically exploiting a child in custody proceedings in the media. The second part satirised Reid's very public, televised comments about Harvey's size.' Channel 4 said 'the joke plays on a classic Oedipus complex in modern day form, with Jordan as the target of the joke' and 'it's well documented that within her own TV series, Ms Price is very physical with her children, especially with Harvey, and the notion of Harvey attacking her is an absurd extreme of that'.

Ofcom noted the importance

attached to freedom of expression in the broadcasting environment. In particular, broadcasters must be permitted to enjoy the creative freedom to explore controversial and challenging issues and ideas, and the public must be free to view and listen to those issues and ideas, without unnecessary interference.

However, Ofcom found that 'the material in question appeared to directly target and mock the mental and physical disabilities of a known eight year-old child who had not himself chosen to be in the public eye. As such, Ofcom found that the comments had considerable potential to be highly offensive to the audience.' It considered that:

even taking into account contextual factors such as the nature of the series as a whole, its scheduling, publicity and the clear pre-transmission warning, these comments went beyond what would have been expected by the majority of viewers of a late night comedy show broadcast on Channel 4.

The material was therefore found to have breached the Ofcom Broadcasting Code.

On 8 December 2010 ATVOD received a complaint about the same programme, including the comments about Harvey Price quoted above, available on the 4oD service. Given the limited rules at ATVOD's disposal, as discussed above, it could only consider whether this was 'material which might seriously impair the physical, mental or moral development of persons under the age of eighteen'. ATVOD's finding explained:

ATVOD recognises that many viewers may regard the material as highly offensive, including to people with disabilities, and unsuitable for under 18s, but providing such content to under 18s is not a breach of the Rules if it does not fall foul of the 'might seriously impair' test.

The provision of the material was therefore found not to constitute a breach of ATVOD's rules.

This case reveals the wide disparity between the regulation of the same programme under the comprehensive Broadcasting Code, and its regulation under the ATVOD rules that are far closer to potential obligations under criminal law. It is important to note that, under the current regulatory framework for on demand services, it is open to commissioners to originate content for video on demand services that is not therefore subject to any impartiality or other harm and offence requirements and, in addition, to repeat polemical stances without the rebroadcast of companion, alternative, viewpoints that provide for impartiality.

This minimal framework throws into question how far the regulation of video on demand services is in line with consumer expectations. If new commissions and/or services exploit the minimal demands of ATVOD in order to provide partial and other content that could not be broadcast under the Ofcom Code, will consumers understand the limits of the regulation for VOD?

Qualitative research for Ofcom on audience perceptions of video on demand, *Regulation of Video on Demand* by Essential, published 18 December 2009 (and further examined in Chapter 7 below) revealed:

Most participants were not aware that broadcaster online catch-up services could show content that had not already been broadcast ... there was a general assumption that all content on such services was already subject to regulation.[140]

Currently, this assumption is not far from mainstream practice. Mainstream providers are voluntarily adopting far greater consumer-facing standards than those required by ATVOD. They provide classification, labelling of content, and PIN protections across both their scheduled and video on demand services and are providing programming that has previously been subject to the Ofcom Broadcasting Code. But, ironically, here lies the rub. If consumers make assumptions that video on demand content is subject to the same standards as scheduled broadcast material, and are cushioned by mechanisms and practices currently applied by familiar mainstream brands, how can they have a clear appreciation of the minimum requirements that are actually required, and enforced, across the full range of video on demand providers? How can they navigate video on demand content as it develops, for example in the realms of news and current affairs, and properly understand what their expectations of it should be? As Pete Johnson observed:

Clearly one of the challenges for both service providers, and regulators of those services, is to address the confusion that may arise in consumers' minds, as to how much protection they can expect as they move seamlessly on their living room television between material that is regulated under the Broadcasting Code, material that is regulated under the ATVOD rules, and material that is not regulated at all because the provider is outside of

---

[140] http://stakeholders.ofcom.org.uk/binaries/research/tv-research/vod.pdf.

jurisdiction.[141] That is going to happen. It may be that consumers manage those transitions seamlessly and happily. It may be that some consumers find that a very jarring leap.

At the moment the impact of the technology is being masked, to some extent, by the voluntary controls that the major VOD providers are putting in place. So obviously most VOD viewing is through the iPlayer so all the content is BBC content that has been complied for television anyway. You're not getting more extreme content. Similarly, the other major providers have put in place their own controls which mean that the limits of what's allowed under the regulations are not being tested in the services that most people are using most of the time at the moment.[142]

As Johnson pointed out, the potential for confusion is most acute with the advent of internet-connected television. Voluntary PIN protections and labelling currently mask the contrast between Ofcom rules for scheduled television and ATVOD rules for video on demand material. However, in Johnson's view:

That's bound to break down, especially when you get more open platforms, and as the TV set in the living room is increasingly linked up to the internet more generally, and services are provided directly into that without an intermediary, it's bound to be the case that some consumers are going to struggle to understand that 'OK, now I'm entering the unregulated world'. At the moment I think when people put on their PC they largely recognise that they are entering an unregulated world, but I think there's still an expectation around the living room TV set that that's something I don't need to worry about. And I don't think we've started to really understand how consumers are going to respond to that.

And there's further complexity in relation to the BBC. BBC iPlayer is available as a standalone service but can also appear on different platforms. If the BBC retains editorial responsibility, then the video on demand material is regulated by the Trust. In the (unlikely) event that the BBC were to cede responsibility to a third party then it would fall under ATVOD regulation. Regulatory requirements are different again for the BBC's commercial arm, BBC Worldwide, as Johnson explained:

Where BBC Worldwide has got the rights to the programmes, and is exploiting the programmes, not through iPlayer, but by agreements with third party platforms, perhaps launching their own platforms, then those protections don't apply because BBC Worldwide doesn't benefit from the carve out that the BBC gets.

This is far from cut and dried however. At the time of writing, BBC Worldwide is contesting ATVOD's determination that its service Top Gear YouTube[143] falls within ATVOD's scope. Its appeal to Ofcom included the argument that this YouTube channel provides only short clips. ATVOD, however, argued that this was not a bar to it falling within its scope.

---

[141] Johnson explained that audiovisual material may be subject to: Ofcom's Broadcasting Code, another EU member state's Broadcasting Code, ATVOD's VOD rules, another EU member state's VOD rules, BBC regulation, or be 'outside jurisdiction' (e.g. services operated from the USA).

[142] Interview May 2011.

[143] http://www.youtube.com/topgear.

Linked to such complexity are questions about how the consumer identifies which of the many regulatory authorities are responsible for specific complaints, and how consumers can have any clear understanding of what their expectations should be of particular services, beyond associations they may make with established brands.[144] Here it is argued that the solution to the issue of consumer confidence is transparency, and future regulation can only be determined by difficult choices over what it is we value in 'the public space' and decisions over what should therefore be required in relation to standards across media platforms. As Pete Johnson explained, some European countries have placed more onerous requirements on providers, including a watershed for video on demand material:

> Quite a number of other EU member states have gold plated the regulations in terms of requirements on labelling. France has requirements to label audio visual content and also imposes watersheds for VOD for content that wouldn't need to be put behind access controls under the Directive. It's also true that other countries have taken a much more active role in ensuring that service providers promote and provide access to European works. For example, France requires certain providers to invest a certain proportion of their global revenues, it requires quotas and imposes a 2% tax on all VOD revenue.[145]

French regulation provides a useful counterpoint to the market-led approach, with its bias against intervention, illustrated in the United States case study discussed in Chapter 3. France demonstrates an interventionist approach to broadcasting regulation, defined by particular cultural objectives.

France: an interventionist approach

Freedom of the press in France is guaranteed and not subject to a statutory regulator. However privacy laws under France's civil code,[146] combined with cultural pressures, do not allow, for example, the same public interest defence used by journalists in the UK in relation to the private lives of politicians.[147] Broadcasting is subject to statutory regulation, as is video on demand content.[148]

As Robert McKenzie notes in his comparison of French and American media regulation, the history of French broadcasting explains a very different approach to the United States discussed in Chapter 3 above:

> For decades, all broadcast media were exclusively owned, operated and regulated by the national government. But after 1982, the National Assembly ... opened up the possibility for broadcast media to be owned and operated by private companies ... [This] situation in which the government regulates culture on both public and private television and for radio broadcasters is a defining feature of the media system in France.[149]

---

[144] See Annex 2 for the House of Lords Select Committee table on complaint handling across BBC and non-BBC services.
[145] Interview May 2011.
[146] http://www.legifrance.gouv.fr/html/codes_traduits/code_civil_textA.htm.
[147] http://www.channel4.com/news/strauss-kahn-scandal-could-change-french-law.
[148] The European Journalism Centre provides briefings on media and regulatory bodies for each European country, set out at http://www.ejc.net/media_landscape.
[149] Robert McKenzie, *Comparing Media Regulation between France, the USA, Mexico and Ghana*, http://www.juridicas.unam.mx/publica/rev/comlawj/cont/6/arc/arc5.htm.

Broadcasting is regulated by the Conseil Supérieur de L´Audiovisuel (CSA), established in 1989, responsible for licensing and enforcement, with sanctions including fines and broadcasting findings. Unlike the oversight of the FCCs by committees whose duties relate to commerce, the 'primary oversight body for the CSA is the Culture Ministry'.[150] Both public and private radio and television stations are subject to public service obligations, in relation to providing a plurality of political voices across services, the protection of minors (including a watershed in relation to sexual and violent material), and protection of programming of French origin. It also regulates for investment in French-originated video on demand material.

As with the press, privacy (particularly in relation to politicians) is a concern for the CSA. In May 2011, in the wake of the arrest of IMF chief Dominique Strauss-Kahn on charges of attempted rape, it issued a warning to broadcasters in relation to images of 'a handcuffed person'.[151] In effect, Article 9.1 of the Civil Code[152] contains a prohibition on the 'infringement of the presumption of innocence' which the CSA held such images would contravene.

This interventionist approach has spilled over into France's approach to video on demand material where it takes broadcasting regulation as its starting point and looks for consistency across platforms. The CSA's 2010 Annual Report explains:

> For the industry, and the regulator, the continued growth in new internet services brings far-reaching change. The Conseil's regulation, therefore, now takes into account on-demand audiovisual media services, such as catch-up TV, or vide- on-demand.[153]

From December 2010 the CSA has applied rules relating to the protection of young audiences and ethics to video on demand content. A watershed applies to video on demand content as well as to scheduled television services and 'only allows content rated +18 and +16 [to] be made available between 22:30 and 05:00'.[154] It also regulates for investment in French-originated video on demand material.

The UK has not added to the basic video on demand regulations and has restricted the formal rules to the specific requirements of the AVMS Directive. On the other hand, Eve Salomon noted that the UK has significantly gold-plated the AVMS Directive when it comes to broadcast television, compared with other countries, applying a comprehensive statutory framework that goes far beyond the minimal AVMS Directive rules for television set out in Chapter 3 above. This, she argued, contrasts sharply with its minimalist approach to applying the AVMS Directive to video on demand material:

> 'What hasn't been thought out is the segue from traditional broadcasting to really converged viewing and regulatory issues around that.'

In reality, therefore, important questions remain unanswered over the nature and level of regulation that should be transparently required of video on demand material by contrast to programming subject to the Ofcom Broadcasting Code. And in addition to broadcasting content providers, new services are providing, or being deemed by ATVOD to provide, video on demand, as will now be explored.

[150] Ibid.
[151] http://www.csa.fr/actualite/communiques/communiques_detail.php?id=133507.
[152] http://www.legifrance.gouv.fr/html/codes_traduits/code_civil_textA.htm.
[153] http://www.csa.fr/rapport2010/summary/building.htm.
[154] http://stakeholders.ofcom.org.uk/binaries/internet/explicit-material-vod.pdf.

5.3. Newspapers and other providers contest ATVOD's authority

Two issues bedevilled ATVOD in its first year: first the fees payable to ATVOD by providers of video on demand services, amounting to an annual levy of £2,900, attracted howls of protest from smaller providers and a statement from ATVOD that it would consider exceptional reasons for a lower tariff in the case of small-scale providers.[155]

The second area of contention is over which services fall within ATVOD's remit. The key features of an 'on-demand programme service' falling within ATVOD regulation are set out in the amended Communications Act. A service is subject to ATVOD regulation if it meets all the following criteria: it includes TV-like programmes (with form and content comparable to television programme services); it is a video on demand service (enabling users to view select programmes when they choose to); there is editorial responsibility (under which the programmes fall) and it is made available to the public (by the person with editorial responsibility).

In sum a service will fall within ATVOD regulation if its principal purpose is to offer 'television-like' content and if it competes for the same audiences as television. ATVOD guidance notes explain that catch-up services, programme archives, and video on demand movie services, where a content aggregator exercises 'editorial responsibility', are likely to be considered services falling under ATVOD regulation. Examples of material not likely to be considered 'on-demand programme services' are non-economic series (not in competition with television broadcasting), services comprising video on demand content that are not 'mass media in their function to inform, entertain and educate the general public', and 'electronic versions of newspapers and magazines (excluding any on-demand programme services offered by newspapers and magazines)'.

Examples of other services excluded are those that provide video content that is: self-generated and posted by private individuals onto video sharing sites with no economic purpose; produced by organisations for their members (rather than for consumption by the general public); or embedded within a text-based editorial article, such as a written news story on a website that contains an illustrative video clip.

Thus electronic versions of newspapers and illustrative clips within text-based editorial articles are excluded, although on demand programme services offered by a newspaper would be caught by ATVOD's regulation. It is here that a tension has arisen in relation to newspapers. As discussed above, since 1997 the PCC has regulated online versions of newspapers and magazines that subscribe to the Editors' Code of Practice (and has more recently extended its remit to audiovisual material on publications' websites, and online-only publications). At the time of the 1997 extension of its remit, the material falling under its jurisdiction was usually an internet replication of material previously published in printed form. However PCC guidance makes clear that:

> the industry recognises that not all material on its titles' websites lends itself to the Code and the jurisdiction of the PCC. Some websites cannot be categorized as 'online versions' of newspapers and magazines. Some material – such as syndicated news broadcasts or radio programmes edited by third parties – may already be regulated online or offline by another body. Some of it may be streamed or broadcast or otherwise disseminated live, and incapable of the sort of controls editors normally apply. Some of it, principally user-generated material such as blogs and chat-rooms, is not subject to editorial control. All such material will continue to fall outside the jurisdiction of the PCC.[156]

---

[155] http://www.atvod.co.uk/uploads/files/VOD_mini-statement_concessionary_fees_-_Further_Final_Version_12112010.pdf.
[156] http://www.pcc.org.uk/assets/111/Audio_Visual_Guidance_Note.pdf.

The PCC confines its remit to

> *covering editorial material on newspaper and magazine titles' websites where it meets two key requirements: 1) that the editor of the newspaper or magazine is responsible for it and could reasonably have been expected both to exercise editorial control over it and apply the terms of the Code. 2) That it was not pre-edited to conform to the on-line or off-line standards of another media regulatory body.*

Media lawyer Siobhain Butterworth, writing in the *Guardian* in March 2011,[157] characterised as a 'land grab' ATVOD's decision to write 'to newspapers, including the *Guardian* and the *Independent*, claiming that they fall within its regulatory ambit'. She continued:

> *Newspapers and the PCC are likely to resist, but if Atvod wins the argument the UK press will, for the first time, be brought under a regulator's control. If not quite regulation by ambush, it may qualify as regulation by stealth ... It is only a skip and a hop from regulation of bits of newspaper websites to regulation of the whole newspaper industry — something that successive governments have shied away from.*

On 21 March 2011 ATVOD announced that News of the World Video, Sun Video, Elle TV, and Sunday Times Video Library were all on demand programme services and would be regulated by ATVOD (unless appeals to Ofcom were successful). Ruth Evans, ATVOD's chair, explained:

> *ATVOD has no desire or remit to regulate the press — whether online or offline — but we do have a duty to be even-handed and apply the new statutory regulations in a fair and consistent manner. Where video content appears as an integral part of an online version of a newspaper, for example, alongside a text based story, then the service falls outside our remit: it is indeed excluded by law. Many services provided by newspapers and magazines fall exactly into this category and can expect to hear nothing from ATVOD. But that is not what happens in these particular services. In each case, a catalogue of 'TV-like' programmes is offered as a discrete service, comparable with many others. There are clear differences between these services and on-line versions of newspapers.[158]*

ATVOD guidance was updated in March 2011 to explain this:

> *There is a difference between (a) an online newspaper offering video reports which supplement and sit alongside text based news stories, and (b) an online newspaper giving over a distinct section of its website to TV-like programmes which have no clear and direct link to the broader 'newspaper' offering and which could exist as a stand alone service.[159]*

---

[157] http://www.guardian.co.uk/law/2011/mar/07/video-self-regulation-press.
[158] http://atvod.co.uk/news-consultations/news-consultationsnews/210311-newspapers.
[159] http://www.atvod.co.uk/uploads/files/Guidance_on_who_needs_to_notify_Ed3.1_Mar_2011.pdf.

Stephen Abell of the PCC argued that it is the statutory back stop powers that underpin ATVOD's co-regulatory remit that the press strenuously resists:

> There is an argument that the PCC could put in its Code two things that would match those two [ATVOD] editorial requirements. But Ofcom have a legal obligation to be backstop to this and so if the PCC were to incorporate this in its Code it would be welcoming Ofcom in as a backstop power to itself. And so the problem the PCC have with ATVOD is not necessarily what it will do because I don't think it will do very much. It's what it is and it is co-regulation which is effectively statutory regulation and that's the problem they have with it. It's statutory regulation of their content in an area where there is no perceivable problem and in areas where they don't feel they will ever come close to breaching.[160]

Ironically he noted that, in order to appeal ATVOD's determination, newspapers 'kind of have to accept Ofcom's jurisdiction' and appeal to Ofcom.

Pete Johnson of ATVOD recognised that one of the AVMS Directive's recitals clearly explains the lack of intention to catch online versions of newspapers in its regulation. However, he argued, this does not allow newspapers to run video on demand services outside of ATVOD regulation:

> We take the view that a website in particular may contain more than one service. It may contain an online version of a newspaper and, sitting alongside that, a video on demand service. And that just because you put it on the same website doesn't necessarily mean it's not a service in its own right. We took the view that the intention of the Directive was to exclude use of video as part of the newspaper but where video is offered in its own discrete section, is aggregated together, is TV-like in its nature and is enjoyed by users without reference to the broader newspaper, it's not really an integral and ancillary part of that newspaper offering, it has become a service in its own right. Now time will tell, the process of appeals will tell, whether in the particular cases on which we have ruled so far, Ofcom agrees with that but I don't think this is something that's going to go away as media owners are straddling television and newspaper.

From a consumer, rather than newspaper industry, perspective the pressing question is what regulation by each body provides. Whether or not ATVOD regulation is eventually required of newspaper video on demand services, the PCC Code will also continue to apply to such services provided by its members.[161] This will provide consumers with a code of standards in relation to video on demand journalism, relating, for example, to accuracy and privacy, which does not apply to other (non-PCC regulated) video on demand services. However, this is on a self-regulatory basis from which newspaper providers can withdraw, and at the time of writing the future of the PCC has yet to be determined.

ATVOD rules, which have a statutory basis, will also apply but offer (as discussed above) only basic provisions whose sufficiency, in relation to protection of children, has been questioned by the Government. And even if both regulatory requirements are imposed, neither is consistent with the comprehensive requirements of Ofcom's

---

[160] Interview May 2011.
[161] Interview Stephen Abell, PCC, May 2011.

Broadcasting Code in respect of both journalism and protection of children (in practice voluntarily adhered to by mainstream video on demand providers as discussed above). While the PCC Code has provisions in relation to interviewing and photographing children, it has no provisions in relation to children as consumers. For Eve Salomon, a former PCC Commissioner, the move by newspaper titles into the provision of audiovisual content raises particular questions about the protections of children and young people:

> There is this hole where it comes to the protection of minors and I suspect that Editors are really going to have to think carefully about adding something about protection of minors into the PCC Code.

For Martin Moore of the Media Standards Trust the quarrel with ATVOD is another blow to the PCC, already struggling, as we have seen, in the wake of the phone-hacking scandal, as well as with the tensions between broadsheets and tabloids and with the loss of credibility as newspaper titles have removed themselves from its jurisdiction:

> The audiovisual situation with ATVOD is quite a serious factor. [The PCC] specifically said two years ago that they would regulate audiovisual content online and ATVOD says "no you won't because we will". So I think they're in a very difficult position. They have no powers, in the sense of no legal powers, so they can't enforce anything.

It is not just newspapers that are contesting ATVOD's jurisdiction. ATVOD's website reveals a number of different providers that ATVOD has determined fall under its scope, but who are appealing that determination to Ofcom as demonstrated in the following case study.

BNPtv: testing ATVOD's jurisdiction

BNPtv, provided by the British National Party, is described by ATVOD as:

> available at http://bnptv.org.uk/ provides access to over 290 programmes which range in length from three minute music videos (eg. 'I see You – By Dave Hannam' [lyrics written by BNP Chairman Nick Griffin]) and news/documentary style short programmes (eg. 'A look back at last year's RWB [Red White and Blue] Festival') to footage of speeches (eg. 'After Dinner Speeches – Bruges', 12 minutes) and longer news style footage (eg. 'Free Speech 2 – The Verdict', 39 minutes).
>   Although some programmes are largely unedited, much is edited into a format which is directly comparable to documentary, current affairs or news programmes normally included in a great number of television programme services, and the content (footage of political events and reports on current affairs) is also directly comparable to the content of programmes normally included in television programme services.[162]

BNPtv disputes ATVOD's determination that it is providing a video on demand service, arguing that the content is 'self-generated and not part of any economic activity'. It faces an enforcement notice, and potential sanction, for rejecting ATVOD's jurisdiction. However, even if it eventually accepts ATVOD's authority, one must again ask where the substantive benefit lies for the citizen and consumer, given the modest nature of

---

[162] http://www.atvod.co.uk/regulated-services/scope-determinations/bnp-tv.

ATVOD's rules. As a notified on demand service provider, partial content from BNPtv could be provided through an internet-connected television without attracting any regulation on accuracy or impartiality.

As described above, BNPtv includes a range of content with the look and feel of documentaries, current affairs, or news programmes. Yet its content has not been previously broadcast and is not therefore subject to the Ofcom Broadcasting Code. As a notified ATVOD service it would be subject to ATVOD's rules on incitement and impairment, discussed above, but beyond that it would be free of regulation whether in relation to accuracy, impartiality, fairness, or privacy.

For those previously unregulated online services there may be resistance (as currently displayed by BNPtv) to coming under ATVOD's authority, since they are currently entirely unregulated and regulation presents a financial burden. On the other hand, for services currently subject to, and periodically breaching, the Ofcom Code, migration to video on demand provision may become a tempting alternative to the burden of Ofcom rules and sanctions.

As we shall see in the next section, regulation of video on demand may also provide a false sense of reassurance to the consumer: implying that broadcast-style standards and protections are in place when these are not, in reality, applicable to video on demand services.

5.4. Video on demand and growth in consumption

While the struggles between ATVOD and newspapers and others are important in the evolving definition of what is, and is not, a video on demand service, they are also a distraction from an important and thus far neglected debate over the value, and potential influence, of video on demand material. As discussed above, the previous self-regulatory code of video on demand providers was dismantled when ATVOD the association became ATVOD the authority, as was the self-regulatory link to Ofcom's comprehensive rules on harm and offence impartiality, privacy, or fairness. The simple justification for this, that we select or 'pull' video on demand material, rather than being 'pushed' it via scheduled, linear television, merits debate and raises a number of further issues.

First, while Ofcom 2010 *Communications Market* report,[163] discussed in Chapter 7 below, shows that scheduled television is still overwhelmingly the most consumed audiovisual medium, it also demonstrates that video on demand consumption is growing (while the number of television channels fell for the first time). As video on demand consumption grows, we must ask how we will continue to justify the approach of 'gold-plating' scheduled linear regulation right through to the least popular nether reaches of the EPG, while requiring such a minimal regulatory framework of increasingly popular video on demand services.

Secondly, the same Ofcom research reveals that the *impact* of selected material is potentially far greater than that of material traditionally seen as 'pushed' at us. Attention levels to a range of activities on computers, television sets and telephones were measured. Downloaded TV and video on demand delivered via a computer attracted amongst the highest levels of attention. On the other hand, watching scheduled television attracted a lower average attention score than most activities, arguing for recognition of the potentially significant impact of on demand content on its consumers.

Thirdly, the research showed that video on demand consumption is growing most rapidly amongst audiences who are younger. This is also illustrated by Channel 4's annual

[163] http://stakeholders.ofcom.org.uk/binaries/research/cmr/753567/CMR_2010_FINAL.pdf. See also http://stakeholders.ofcom.org.uk/binaries/research/cmr/cmr11/UK_CMR_2011_FINAL.pdf.

report for 2010 *Looking Back Looking Forward*,[164] which reported developments in digital media in relation to on demand, self-scheduled, consumption. It reported that online viewing of programmes rose significantly in 2010 on YouTube, channel4.com, and other platforms: 'Across all platforms, 31 million streams of full-length Channel 4 programmes [were] initiated each month on average in 2010; a total of 372 million views over the year.' It also reported investment outside of programming in specialist websites. It said these were 'attracting more than 30 million visits each month on average, equivalent to 360 million visits across the year; a 56% increase on 2009'.

In particular it noted that younger audiences led the '71% increase on 2009' in video on demand viewing:

> *The most popular programmes on our 4oD service were series aimed at younger audiences – The Inbetweeners, Hollyoaks, Big Brother, Skins and Glee. The latest series of The Inbetweeners achieved nearly 8 million views on channel4.com alone across the year, and broke our record for the number of on-demand views of a single episode in a single day. 4oD also proved to be a valuable way of engaging loyal audiences with their favourite content in new ways.*

The generational divide, evidenced by the consumer research in Chapter 7 below, argues for particular consideration for young people, and in particular children, as video on demand consumers who may require particular safeguards. Chapter 10 argues that the inconsistencies in current regulation within and between platforms, justified by notions of 'push' and 'pull', are likely to result in consumer confusion that could undermine confidence in scheduled and video on demand services alike. It argues for a fresh consideration of the public space provided by all services, including video on demand. It considers the role for statutory regulation in providing appropriate standards, and a role for 'independent' regulation (also discussed in relation to the press in Chapter 4).

5.5. Lessons from the platform-neutral approach of ATVOD for wider media regulation

As we have seen, the UK has chosen to take a minimalist approach to the rules for video on demand content, and has instead concentrated on developing the regulatory architecture around it, seeking clearly to define to whom the rules apply, and the requirements of the notification process. This seeks to place the regulation of video on demand material on secure foundations while leaving open the question of how far the rules themselves should be developed or supplemented. What ATVOD provides is a truly platform-neutral regulatory framework that requires that providers notify the Authority that they intend to provide a video on demand programme service and then comply with the rules set out by the Authority. It is perhaps in the architecture of its regulatory framework, rather than the content of its editorial rules, that ATVOD's greatest strength lies as we approach the next Communications Act.

For Eve Salomon, author of the UNESCO/Commonwealth Broadcasting Association Guidelines for Broadcasting Regulation, the logical conclusion is to adopt the same approach to scheduled television as to video on demand:

> *I've actually felt for quite some time that the inevitable outcome is that Ofcom's content obligations, other than in respect of public service broadcasting, will have to be transferred to ATVOD. That seems to me the logical conclusion of where we are going … Given that we're seeing an*

[164] http://www.channel4.com/media/documents/corporate/annual-reports/Ch4_Annual_Report_2010_FINAL.pdf.

increased amount of viewing over the internet, particularly amongst young people, the logical conclusion of that is that the hefty range of standards obligations that apply to traditional broadcasting become ... redundant.[165]

Salomon saw this as an area that is 'ripe for commercial decisions to be taken' rather than for formal regulation. She advocated basic statutory requirements, supplemented by a voluntary regulatory framework, for both scheduled and video on demand content. It is an area considered further below in Chapter 10.

It is notable that there are currently no requirements for on demand radio services, since the Audiovisual Media Services Directive that underpins the ATVOD rules relates only to 'audiovisual', and not to 'audio', content. On demand radio services are subject to no external regulation. Just as in the audiovisual world explored above, mainstream services are providing 'pre-regulated' content (i.e. broadcast material subject to Ofcom's rules) while other providers are not.

The service RadioPlayer was launched by the BBC, Global Radio, Guardian Media Group, Absolute Radio, and RadioCentre in March 2011, and explains it is 'an online audio player which gives you access to live, on demand and podcast radio from hundreds of stations in the UK'.[166] It brings together BBC and UK commercial stations in one internet site and in May 2011 it was reported as receiving 5.7 million unique users and to be extending to all Ofcom-licensed stations by the end of 2011.[167] With no external regulation of radio on demand services, the link to Ofcom licences is significant, as Matt Payton of RadioCentre explained:

> *RadioPlayer itself is not going to judge who is an appropriate provider. What it has said for the time being is that it will only take Ofcom-licensed stations – that's their way around it. They say 'we're not going to judge whether you're an appropriate content provider, Ofcom does that'. That actually also includes community radio, student radio, hospital radio. As long as they are Ofcom licensed they are happy to [have] them on the platform ... I guess the incumbent players, naturally, would err towards that sort of fudge for the time being because it provides them with [a] walled garden with greater access [to audiences].*

However, this fudge in relation to regulation throws up a number of questions: what are citizen expectations in relation to on demand audio content? (Research on video on demand expectations[168] discussed above suggests that consumers would assume it to be subject to broadcasting regulation.) Would content found to be in breach of the Ofcom Code still be provided on RadioPlayer? Will the stations on the service provide originated on demand material that has never been subject to the Ofcom Code? If the material would be subject to scheduling restrictions when broadcast, for example, at times when children are particularly likely to be listening (radio's equivalent to the 9pm watershed for television), is this apparent to parents and children when provided on demand? And how is the consumer to distinguish RadioPlayer from other online, on demand radio content providers, such as tunein which provides 'over 50,000 local, international and Internet stations ... through websites, mobile devices, home entertainment centers, connected desktop products and even auto in-dash receivers',[169] where licensed and unlicensed, regulated and unregulated, stations sit side by side?

[165] Interview May 2011.
[166] http://www.radioplayer.co.uk.
[167] http://www.bbc.co.uk/news/technology-13613537.
[168] http://stakeholders.ofcom.org.uk/binaries/research/tv-research/vod.pdf.
[169] http://tunein.com.

Chapter 10 below discusses a proposed answer to this lack of regulatory coherence: independent regulation of non-public service radio and television providers, for content across platforms, which is readily signalled for the consumer.

6. Regulation of Wider Online Content

The invitation to Dr Eric Schmidt, executive chairman of Google, to give the MacTaggart Lecture at the 2011 Edinburgh International Television Festival[170] nicely illustrates the convergence of the broadcast and online worlds. The executive chair of the festival, Elaine Bedell, commented on the decision to invite Schmidt:

> *This is the first time that the prestigious MacTaggart has been given to someone not principally involved in television broadcast or production. Eric Schmidt will give us a unique perspective on the future of the UK's television industry, as well as an insight into the global ambitions of the internet-based giant, Google.[171]*

The advisory chair of the festival, George Entwistle, called it 'the perfect MacTaggart for an industry at the convergence crossroads'.

In the event Schmidt used the lecture to extend a hand of friendship from Google to television content producers. He heaped praise on the quality of UK production and left his audience in no doubt of the increasing importance of video on demand provision. Schmidt argued, as would be expected, against over-regulation and cited YouTube as an example of a flexible, light-touch, self-regulatory approach to content standards, examined below.

6.1. Online content is largely unregulated but regulation may be 'crowdsourced'

Google-owned YouTube is one of the areas that will be watched with great interest at the 'convergence crossroads'. YouTube content, aside from requirements in relation to video on demand service providers discussed above and below, is largely exempt from regulation. It is still seen principally as a video sharing site for user-generated material and, as with other sites that adopt their own framework of standards, sets out its 'Community Guidelines', based on trust and calling for respect:

> *We're not asking for the kind of respect reserved for nuns, the elderly, and brain surgeons. We mean don't abuse the site. Every cool new community feature on YouTube involves a certain level of trust. We trust you to be responsible, and millions of users respect that trust, so please be one of them.[172]*

---

[170] http://www.guardian.co.uk/media/interactive/2011/aug/26/eric-schmidt-mactaggart-lecture-full-text.
[171] http://www.mgeitf.co.uk/home/news.aspx/dr_eric_schmidt_to_deliver_mactaggart_lecture.
[172] http://www.youtube.com/t/community_guidelines.

YouTube says it 'doesn't allow videos with nudity, graphic violence or hate. If you come across a video like this, click the link on the video to flag it as Inappropriate and submit the form on the next page to report it to YouTube.' It warns that it works closely with law enforcement agencies (for example, in relation to child exploitation). It warns against posting videos of 'bad stuff' (for example, animal abuse, drug abuse, or bomb making), gratuitous violence or humiliation, 'gross-out' videos (accidents, dead bodies), and bans copyright violation, hate speech, and predatory behaviour or invasions of privacy. It warns that violations of its terms of use results in account termination and a prohibition from creating new accounts. While the language takes a rather different approach to the codes and rules discussed above, the requirements are wider than the two ATVOD rules on editorial content in that they extend to, for example, privacy and nudity.

Such 'crowdsourced' regulation, in which everyone is a regulator, relied on to flag material that breaches the guidelines, is, Schmidt argued, the only possible response to the volumes of self-generated material on YouTube:

> *It's important to understand, YouTube is a platform. It isn't practically possible for us to exercise editorial control in the way a TV channel can. If YouTube had to pre-vet every new video – 48 hours every minute – it simply couldn't exist.*

Instead he sought to set out a bottom–up rather than top–down approach to regulation:

> *Alongside the Internet's benefits, there is content and behaviour none of us want to encourage. From copyright infringement to phishing scams to sexual abuse imagery – none of this is good. But when legislators try to figure out how to minimise the harm of online content, technology solutions rather than laws should be their first thought ... policy makers should work with the grain of the Internet rather than against it. Harness the huge levels of user engagement we have online to find solutions. Encourage online innovators to find new ways for parents to protect their kids. A good example is YouTube's Community Guidelines, setting rules for YouTube content that go further than the law and enable users themselves to identify content that's inappropriate and have it taken down.*

However, the effectiveness of this approach has been criticised. The July 2008 report of the Culture, Media and Sport Select Committee on harmful content on the internet[173] was concerned at the lack of proactive screening and shocked by the time taken for the most extreme content to be removed. YouTube's introduction of Safety Mode in 2010 has begun to address concerns over parental controls.

In addition to user-generated material, Google has been reported as seeking to move YouTube into investments in original programming (rather than acquiring expensive rights to existing series). The potential for higher quality original content raises questions about regulatory confusion. Consumers may understand that user-generated content is outside formal regulation but may have different expectations of content with the look and feel of quality programming. As the *Guardian*'s head of media and technology Dan Sabbagh put it:

> *Hook up the television to the internet, and hit YouTube ... and it's ready to watch in all 24 inches. There's no tedious Ofcom regulations about impartiality to worry about either. What's emerging is a growing amount of*

---

[173] http://www.publications.parliament.uk/pa/cm200708/cmselect/cmcumeds/353/35302.htm.

broadcasting outside traditional TV channels ... Hang on, you might shout. Look how popular linear television channels are. Adam Crozier, ITV's chief executive, said that catch-up, internet viewing was only 1% of total viewing. The five main channels account for 56% of total TV viewing – and when stars like Trinny and Susannah go online after losing their own primetime show, they do not necessarily have Beck-like prospects. Yes, for now, this is all true – but then ask which way the trend is going. After all, consider what younger viewers are up to – for example, as Crozier himself noted recently, half of all viewing for that fine programme The Only Way Is Essex is conducted (if that's the right word) online. And consider, too, what would happen if a company like Google/YouTube or AOL/HuffPo decided to invest properly in producing video content.[174]

Eric Schmidt used his MacTaggart speech to outline a future for Google as a content provider not a content producer originating YouTube programming, telling his audience: 'We'll never be in your league when it comes to commissioning and creating content – it's not our skill set and it's not our business.'[175] Whether or not this proves to be the case, already material subject to YouTube's 'Community Guidelines' sits alongside content from traditional broadcasters including the BBC, Channel 4, CBS, NBC, and Fox which is made available under partnership deals with YouTube to showcase clips (often extended, self-contained clips) of their content.

ATVOD's criteria (and rules) for video on demand services apply if the service falls under UK jurisdiction (with a registered office in the UK) and, as explored above, the criteria are platform neutral. YouTube itself, and its main offering of user-generated material, is distinct from third-party services provided on it, as Pete Johnson explained:

We have looked at all the YouTube channels to see if they are video on demand programme services. Many of them are not, because they don't meet all the criteria, but some of them are clearly video on demand programme services. 4oD operates on the YouTube platform and we think there's a complete distinction from that – where a service provider is using YouTube as a platform – and the main YouTube offering which is to be a platform for users to upload their own material and share it. So we draw a very big distinction between those two.[176]

As demonstrated by the example of BBC Worldwide Top Gear Service, above, ATVOD considers some services providing short clips on YouTube to fall within its regulation. Long-form YouTube services such as 4oD which can be accessed via Channel 4's website[177] and YouTube[178] are already ATVOD notified services.

Indeed Schmidt also observed:

YouTube now has long-form content thanks to pioneering partners like Channel 4, who in 2009 became the first broadcaster in the world to put up their full catch-up service. Long-form is the fastest growing YouTube category in the UK both in terms of views and revenues, now with more than 80 content partners.

---

[174] http://www.guardian.co.uk/media/organgrinder/2011/apr/11/online-television-channels-regulation.

[175] http://www.mgeitf.co.uk/home/news.aspx/dr_eric_schmidt_to_deliver_mactaggart_lecture.

[176] Interview May 2011.

[177] http://www.channel4.co/programmes/4oD.

[178] http://www.youtube.com/user/4oD.

This juxtaposition of well-known brands like Channel 4 on a platform with other video on demand services as well as user-generated material raises questions over consumer expectations. The general starting point among consumers (as discussed in Chapter 7 below) is that the internet is unregulated. However, with some video on demand material subject to ATVOD's rules, some to BBC Trust regulation, some to voluntary codes, that assumption is thrown into question. In the case of YouTube the question for UK consumers, as they navigate their way through programming provided by the third most popular site on the planet (after Google and Facebook), is identifying whether content is subject to gold-plated, rudimentary, or any regulation.

Chapter 9 below considers mechanisms that could 'tag' content and signal regulation in order to enable consumers clearly to identify regulated material.

6.2. Bloggers resist suggestions of PCC regulation

From the largest to the smallest online media provider, standards regulation has been steadily progressing up the agenda. Bloggers went into a flat spin over suggestions in November 2009 that the then recently appointed Chair of the Press Complaints Commission was intending to extend the PCC's remit to cover blogs. The *Independent*'s Iain Burrell had reported Baroness Buscombe as saying:

> Some of the bloggers are now creating their own ecosystems which are quite sophisticated ... Is the reader of those blogs assuming that it's news, and is [the blogosphere] the new newspapers? It's a very interesting area and quite challenging.[179]

Burrell reported her as telling him 'she would want the organisation to "consider" whether it should seek to extend its remit to the blogosphere'.

Iain Dale's blog response was typical of fierce resistance by bloggers to what was seen to be the suggestion of required regulation:[180]

> We might write the same bollocks as newspaper journalists, but we don't get paid for it, for a start. Many of us do not see ourselves as primarily news outlets, either. I'd estimate that ninety per cent of my content could loosely be described as comment. I see absolutely no need for independently operated blogs to be regulated by the PCC or indeed anyone else. If they want to propose a voluntary system of regulation, fine. But the day they try to mandate it is the day I will give up blogging.

A letter was despatched from Liberal Conspiracy blog[181] to the PCC declaring:

> While we are grateful for your interest in our activities we must regretfully decline your kind offer of future PCC regulation. Frankly, we do not feel that the further development of blogging as an interactive medium that facilitates the free exchange of ideas and opinions will benefit from regulation by a body representing an industry with, in the main, substantially lower ethical standards and practices than those already practiced by the vast majority of established British bloggers.

[179] http://ianburrell.independentminds.livejournal.com/8357.html.
[180] http://iaindale.blogspot.com/2009/11/pcc-chairwoman-wants-to-regulate-blogs.html.
[181] http://liberalconspiracy.org/2009/11/17/blogging-and-pcc-regulation-a-collective-response/ also
http://www.guardian.co.uk/media/greenslade/2009/nov/18/peta-buscombe-pcc.

It continued:

> We would suggest that before you even consider turning your attention to our activities, you should direct your energies towards putting your own house in proper order. Should you succeed in raising the ethical standards and practices of the majority of the national press, particularly the tabloids, to our level then we may be inclined to reconsider our position. Until that happens, any attempt by the Press Complaints Commission to regulate the activities of bloggers will be strenuously resisted at every possible turn.

Lady Buscombe subsequently confirmed that any such regulation would be voluntarily undertaken when she responded that blogging

> is a clear area where freedom of expression is absolutely paramount. I have no desire to infringe on that. My point was that, as there is already pressure to increase regulation of the internet, it is important to make clear that this must not lead to some form of statutory interference. Rather, a system of self-regulation (such as exists by the PCC for newspapers) would be more appropriate, if any bloggers wished to go down that route.[182]

For a blogger wishing to go down this route, the following case study illustrates how the PCC's Editors' Code works in practice for blogs that already fall under its regulation, and how it could work as a voluntary code extended to bloggers more widely.

PCC case study: Spectator blog

Rod Liddle became the first blogger to be found in breach of the Editors' Code following a blog he posted on *The Spectator* magazine's website on 5 December 2009:[183]

> The first of an occasional series – those benefits of a multi-cultural Britain in full. Let me introduce you all to this human filth [Here Liddle inserted a link to a Mail Online report about two black rappers 'who tried to murder a pregnant 15-year-old girl for getting in the way of their careers' and were jailed for a total of 32 years[184]]. It could be an anomaly, of course. But it isn't. The overwhelming majority of street crime, knife crime, gun crime, robbery and crimes of sexual violence in London is carried out by young men from the African-Caribbean community. Of course, in return, we have rap music, goat curry and a far more vibrant and diverse understanding of cultures which were once alien to us. For which, many thanks.

Following a complaint that challenged the blog's assertion that young African-Caribbean men were responsible for the 'overwhelming majority' of such crime, the PCC investigated under clause 1 of its Code on Accuracy.[185] It said the complainant had referred to Ministry of Justice statistics demonstrating that, in offences of violence against the person and sexual offences for example, black people made up 32% of arrests.

The Spectator offered evidence to substantiate the crime figures in the posting and, significantly, also sought to argue that the blog was a substantially different medium to print journalism. It said that

[182] http://liberalconspiracy.org/2009/11/19/the-pcc-still-want-to-regulate-blogs-the-baroness-responds.

[183] http://www.spectator.co.uk/rodliddle/5601833/benefits-of-a-multicultural-britain.thtml.

[184] http://www.dailymail.co.uk/news/article-1233207/Pregnant-teen-thrown-canal-rappers-plotted-murder-internet-chatroom.html.

[185] http://www.pcc.org.uk/cases/adjudicated.html?article=NjMxNg==.

blogging was a conversational medium in which readers were able to disagree with the writer's opinion immediately, as had happened in this case. In that sense, the piece as a whole had been written by the columnist and those who had commented. In addition, it had published a separate blog by another author in which the accuracy of the claim was called into question.

The PCC said it recognised that 'the nature of a blog post is often provocative and conducive to discussion', however, the magazine had not been able to substantiate its claim in relation to members of the African-Caribbean community being responsible for the 'overwhelming majority' of crime referred to in the blog. It noted that rather than being presented as the columnist's opinion:

it was a statement of fact. As such, the Commission believed that the onus was on the magazine to ensure that it was corrected authoritatively online. It could not rely merely on the carrying of critical reaction to the piece.

The complaint was upheld and *The Spectator* published the full PCC adjudication,[186] prompting months of comments posted by those following the blog. The PCC clearly did not accept the magazine's 'conversational medium' argument and judged the blog against precisely the same tests as any print article, namely the requirement 'not to publish inaccurate, misleading or distorted information'. Questions of harm and offence, including impartiality, were not at issue.

For Paul Bradshaw who publishes the Online Journalism Blog,[187] there are problems with the notion of any regulatory framework for bloggers. While he acknowledged that a self-regulatory code could play its part in demonstrating trustworthiness, he argued that it could equally smack of 'sell-out' to the mainstream:

people draw on a range of 'signals' to make a judgement about the trustworthiness of [blogging] content: that includes their personal history of interactions with the author; the author's formal credentials, including qualifications and employer; the author's network; the author's behaviour with others; numerous other factors including for example ratings by strangers, friends ... and of course the content itself – is the evidence transparent, the argument /narrative logical, etc. A self-regulatory Code would add another signal – but one that could be interpreted either way: some will see it as a badge of credibility; others as a badge of 'sell-out' or pretence to authority.[188]

Rather, he argued, the standards to which a blogger adheres are woven into his or her wider 'social capital'. Unlike traditional notions of reputation, Bradshaw pointed to the way in which such content is part of a conversation with a network of others who post responses, continue debates, and rate its value – all of which provides an indication of ethical standards and of trustworthiness:

my accuracy, fairness and treatment of the vulnerable dictates part of my social capital. If I make a mistake, my social capital can be damaged for a long time to come – we don't yet have any concept of our social crimes 'expiring' online.

---

[186] http://www.spectator.co.uk/essays/all/5874173/pcc-adjudication-on-rod-liddles-blogpost-benefits-of-a-multicultural-britain.thtml.
[187] onlinejournalismblog.com.
[188] Email interview May 2011.

Thirdly, he argued, even if a self-regulatory code were up for discussion, association with the PCC would, as demonstrated by bloggers' reactions above, be extremely problematic:

> *Many people blog precisely because they feel that the press does not self-regulate effectively: in a sense they are competing with the PCC (one academic described bloggers as 'Estate 4.5'[189]). It has a bad reputation – to stand any chance of attracting bloggers it would have to give them a genuine voice and incorporate many of the ethical concerns that they have about journalism. I don't see that happening.*

Bradshaw's comments are useful in separating any easy associations between regulation of content, on the one hand, and trust in it, on the other. However, transparency is, as he notes, at the heart of trustworthiness. Concerns have surfaced over a lack of transparency in relation to bloggers' commercial interests in products, for example, new technologies they endorse, and a 'revolving door' between journalism and industry as writers switch between independent journalism and corporate communications.[190] Some reviewers of technology products and developments have established 'ethics statements', codifying their values into a statement not professing objective impartiality, but rather a declaration of independent subjectivity. Walt Mossberg, co-editor of AllThingsD.com, a website owned by NewsCorp's Dow Jones, and offering news, analysis, and opinion on technology, the internet, and media, writes in his ethics statement:

> *I am not an objective news reporter, and am not responsible for business coverage of technology companies. I am a subjective opinion columnist, a reviewer of consumer technology products and a commentator on technology issues ... I don't accept any money, free products, or anything else of value, from the companies whose products I cover, or from their public relations or advertising agencies. I also don't accept trips, speaking fees, or product discounts from companies whose products I cover, or from their public relations or advertising agencies. I don't serve as a consultant to any companies, or serve on any corporate boards or advisory boards.[191]*

He and his fellow columnists provide declarations of interests, and their content is subject to the comments and conversations of readers' postings. As Stephen Abell of the PCC observed, the notion of trust itself has been transformed with the advent of social media and the engagement it enables:

> *What does trust mean? Does it imply some sort of nannying or do people want to have a more robust engagement with the media? No one trusts anything unquestioningly any more. The era of cynicism is here. Fifty years ago you trusted your doctor, you trusted the policeman, now that era of deference has gone and, particularly in the media, people question the manner of communication all the time. And that means you're not going to trust the media, you don't see it as a monolithic institution giving you information. You see it as something that you engage with, you write back to, you blog about, you comment at the end of articles. That sort of*

---

[189] Jane B. Singer, 'Journalists and News Bloggers: Complements, Contradictions, and Challenges', in Axel Bruns and Joanne Jacobs (eds), *Uses of Blogs* (New York: Peter Lang, 2006).
[190] http://www.mondaynote.com/2011/09/11/the-blogosphere%E2%80%99s-soft-corruption.
[191] http://allthingsd.com/20110907/digital-folio-review-online-shopping-on-the-side/#walt-ethics.

democratisation of the process I think would lead necessarily to a drop in deference. You wrestle with it on your own terms rather than being a passive consumer.[192]

Abell argued that self-regulation is part of the very fabric of online conversations, given the way in which comment builds on comment, and is thus a good fit for the online world:

The Code can apply in this area in a similar way as it can off-line. And indeed online is a medium that responds well to self regulation because it's immediate, if a problem arises it can be addressed quickly. One of the functions of the PCC has always been to have things taken down, things being amended, concerns being sent to the person straight away. All of those things fit the online world. And there is an argument that online is a naturally self-regulating medium. Even leaving aside formal bodies like the PCC – blogs have comments, you can have a conversation, respond to your readers. The freedom of expression that underpins it is one that fits self regulation as a philosophy rather well.

Since the beginning of 2010 the PCC has offered an 'open invitation' to online news providers voluntarily to sign up to the PCC Code. Stephen Abell sees the notion of accreditation, linked to ethical standards and therefore to trust in journalism, as providing significant appeal to online journalists. Whatever the future of the PCC, the notion of accreditation is one that could usefully inform future press regulation.

6.3. A key driver towards regulation for online content may be accreditation

The added value derived from regulation is an area the PCC has been keen to promote in order to differentiate its members' content from providers (including Express Newspapers) that do not accept its jurisdiction. Extended to online-only providers, this could also serve to differentiate self-regulated from unregulated content providers.

At the end of each page the *Sun*'s website carries the message 'The Sun website is regulated by the Press Complaints Commission' and a live link to the PCC's website. Johnson Press does the same with its titles, for example, below each page of the *Edinburgh Evening News* is the statement: 'This newspaper adheres to the PCC Code of Practice', together the PCC's logo and web link.

However, Abell was clear that this does not suggest 'approved' content, rather it has been applied as a mark of standards or accreditation. It is, he argued, a notion that fits with the broadening of regulation of newspaper online material to include certain twitter accounts. It also fits with attempts by other bodies to discriminate between 'professional' and 'amateur' journalists. In February 2011 the Lord Chief Justice's consultation[193] opened, asking how the use of live, text-based communications (twitter, email, and text messages) from court could be permitted for the purposes of 'fair and accurate reporting' by the media. The issue of who is to be classified as 'the media' was raised, and acknowledged to be rapidly developing:

---

[192] Interview May 2011.
[193] http://www.judiciary.gov.uk/Resources/JCO/Documents/Consultations/cp-live-text-based-forms-of-comms.pdf.

the identity of those wishing to participate in reporting is evolving with the technology by which those events are reported. Student newspapers, bloggers and social commentators may wish to engage in live, text-based communications from court, but would not necessarily have media accreditation.

It argued:

Non-accredited members of the media cannot be presumed to have the same appreciation of the legal framework surrounding court reporting, or the industry standards set out by the Press Complaints Commission, as accredited media representatives must be presumed to have.

Accreditation could prove to be a key determinant in deciding who will be considered eligible to engage in live, text-based court reporting. The notion of regulation as a mark of accreditation was one that Stephen Abell was keen to develop, in order to differentiate its members' content, commenting when interviewed:

We're expanding the remit of the PCC to include certain twitter accounts. So if you're a journalist and working from an account that mentions you work from 'x' paper, but is not editorially controlled by that paper, the PCC would not wish to be involved in that ... If it's The Times newsdesk's twitter feed, or an officially appointed representative of the paper in the manner in which they tweet, then I think people would have a regulatory expectation of that. If that's what happens then again it's this notion of accreditation which might lead to the court saying you [an accredited journalist] may tweet from court but you, Mr Blogger, may not. How fair that is and how maintainable as more bloggers become more powerful and part of the system is an interesting question.[194]

The notion of accreditation has been developed by other countries struggling with distinctions between 'professional' and 'amateur' or 'citizen' journalists, as the following developments in Canada and Australia demonstrate.

Canada and Australia: defining the status of 'professional' journalists in a converged media landscape

In Canada, the Quebec Government has established a task force, the Working Group on the Future of Journalism and Information in Quebec, to consider possible ways forward. Its first report, by former journalist Dominique Payette and published in January 2011,[195] concluded that legislation was needed to ensure that the public 'continue to benefit from high-quality information, a foundation of democracy and citizen participation' and so that 'the supply of information and the conditions of practicing professional journalism do not deteriorate further'. She recommended the adoption of a law on the status of 'professional journalists'. This would distinguish 'professionals' from 'amateurs' (such as bloggers and citizen journalists). Professional status would confer certain privileges, for example, in relation to court reporting and access to information, and eligibility for tax credits or Quebec Government subsidy; membership would be mandatory for all news organisations in the Quebec Press Council;[196] and the Press Council itself would be

[194] Interview May 2011.
[195] http://www.mcccf.gouv.qc.ca/fileadmin/documents/publications/rapport-Payette-2010.pdf.
[196] http://www.conseildepresse.qc.ca.

strengthened with the power to draw up a common code of ethics and impose sanctions.

In August 2011 Quebec's Minister of Culture, Communications and the Status of Women, Christine St-Pierre, launched a public consultation[197] asking whether the status of professional journalists should be recognised and if so how it would be determined, by whom, and whether it should be linked to privileges including, for example, privileged access to court and government information. The consultation and the Payette Report on which it is based are controversial, bringing with them associations of licensing of the press and a concern that citizen journalists would be given a 'second-class' status rather than being encouraged to flourish.[198] However, they also raise useful notions of incentivising standards for journalism and conferring public recognition on them.

At the same time the Australian Government has been carrying out a consultation on convergence.[199] Its Convergence Review was launched in December in 2010 'to examine the changes in media and communications caused by the convergence of older technologies such as television with the internet' and, following a preliminary public consultation, published an *Emerging Issues Paper.*[200] The paper discussed 'regulatory parity' and the logic of a policy framework that 'can develop around a specific service regardless of its mode of delivery'.

It noted that 'The concept of regulatory parity has appeal for many stakeholders although stakeholders may differ on whether it is best achieved by deregulating services or by regulating services that currently have little or no regulation.'

Currently radio and television in Australia is subject to statutory regulation by the Australian Communications and Media Authority (ACMA), while the press is self-regulated by the Australian Press Council (APC). News Corporation title *The Australian* reported that the APC was 'developing plans to regulate news and current affairs commentary across all platforms, including radio, television and blogs', quoting its chairman Julian Disney as saying it was 'silly and unworkable to have regulatory processes that differ between various formats, platforms and devices' and 'It makes more sense to have a unified body to adjudicate on these matters – not one divided by media or platform'.

On the issue of accreditation he was quoted as observing 'If rights and privileges are given to people who are journalists, then bloggers – those who take on those rights and privileges – should have to comply with the same things that traditional journalists need to comply with.'[201]

For the UK the same questions, as discussed above, have emerged from the 2011 consultation on court reporting. They go to the heart of how citizens are to distinguish and evaluate credible sources of information; how bodies such as governments and the courts are to engage with journalists; how journalists and publications with different values and ambitions may seek to differentiate themselves; and the role, in each of these challenges, of publicly agreed journalistic standards.

Going forward, whatever the future shape of press regulation following the Leveson Inquiry, the notion of accreditation, linked to preferential access to material, could clearly incentivise some online journalists to demonstrate their commitment to fair and accurate reporting, whether on blogs or Twitter. For others, the value of Twitter and other social networking sites is that they are unregulated, as demonstrated by the information relating to super injunctions released on such sites.

[197] www.mcccf.gouv.qc.ca/consultation.
[198] http://www.nationalpost.com/Quebec+mulls+privileged+professional+journalists/5297817/story.html.
[199] http://www.dbcde.gov.au/digital_economy/convergence_review.
[200] www.dbcde.gov.au/_data/assets/pdf_file/0020/137270/Convergence_Review_Emerging_Issues_paper_PDF,_707_KB.pdf.
[201] http://www.theaustralian.com.au/business/media/regulator-plans-to-expand-powers/story-e6frg996-1226119248754.

Chapter 10 considers how far new and existing content providers could be incentivised to seek regulation on a voluntary basis, and how far this would assist consumers in navigating online content. It does not propose detaching news and current affairs from other content for the purposes of regulation as suggested in the Australian coverage (although Chapter 9 recognises this as an option in the long term). Rather it proposes a framework that manages transition from regulating content according to its mode of distribution (broadcast, print, video on demand) to an approach that seeks to differentiate between the values and commitments of different providers.

6.4. Standards requirements for online public service content

As discussed above, the PCC has proactively extended its remit from print to online and to certain Twitter accounts. Its active solicitation of new members beyond traditional newspaper titles demonstrates the responsiveness of its approach to new media (even if responsibility for video on demand is still to be determined with ATVOD) and its flexibility in expanding the application of its Editors' Code. By contrast, application of Ofcom's Broadcasting Code, reflecting its statutory duties, remains restricted to its licensed linear, scheduled services, and the ATVOD rules are restricted to video on demand services.

However, Ofcom's broader duties have been extended across platforms. The Digital Economy Act 2010, although most widely associated with its clauses on online infringement of copyright, was interesting in its extension of our understanding of public service content from traditional scheduled, linear television and radio to online services.

First it extended Ofcom's duties to review and report on the fulfilment of public service objectives by media services. It set out that 'media services' are not just television and radio services, but also on demand programme services and 'other services provided by means of the internet where there is a person who exercises editorial control over the material included in the service'.[202] The Act therefore recognised that public service objectives extend across current platforms.

Secondly, the Act amended Channel 4's functions, stating 'C4C [Channel 4 Television Corporation] must, in particular, participate in ... the broadcasting or distribution of relevant media content by means of a range of different types of electronic communications networks'.[203] As Ed Vaizey, the Minister for Culture, Communications and Creative Industries, put it on 31 January 2011 in a letter to the Culture Media and Sport Committee:[204]

> The Digital Economy Act 2010, set out new provisions to introduce new accountability arrangements for C4C, that includes a role for Ofcom. These new provisions recognised that the way in which audiences consume audiovisual content and services has been transformed by digital and online technologies. The Act amended the role of C4C; they are now able to provide public service content on all their channels and platforms rather than being restricted to the traditional linear TV model. Decisions about the most appropriate platform for specific content and services will be a matter for C4C, subject to Ofcom's guidance.[205]

---

[202] http://www.legislation.gov.uk/ukpga/2010/24/section/2.
[203] http://www.legislation.gov.uk/ukpga/2010/24/section/22.
[204] http://www.publications.parliament.uk/pa/cm201011/cmselect/cmcumeds/891/89104.htm.
[205] Ofcom guidance note on Channel 4's statement of programme and media content policy was subsequently published on 15 Feb. 2011: http://stakeholders.ofcom.org.uk/binaries/broadcast/guidance/c4c-guidance-note.pdf.

No mention however is made of the different *standards* regimes operating across platforms. These regimes, as demonstrated in the Frankie Boyle case study above, allow for a public service provider's content to breach regulation when provided on a scheduled, linear service, but to be permitted on demand; they prohibit misleading and impartial content on linear television, while allowing it on demand; they also lack transparency for the consumer, as Chapter 7 suggests. The recognition of cross-platform public service content is helpful, but it must be matched by consistent standards regulation signalling that such content is accountable and deserving of public confidence.

There is a further role for public service providers as their functions extend to online provision, and this relates to unease over the ability of the internet to reinforce prejudices. Peter Horrocks articulated this concern in a lecture for the Reuters Institute for the Study of Journalism in November 2006:[206]

> *Tailored news services, internet TV and radio stations, blogs and other new interactive services now offer various minority segments and interest groups news that cater for highly specialist tastes. Those niche services offer their audiences information that often has the effect of re-enforcing their prejudices. There has always been a desire from parts of the audience to have news information that validates their prior values. Newspapers in the UK have, after all, had pretty clear political and social perspectives. But in the electronic media it is only relatively recently that this type of news, predominantly through the internet, has been widely available. My strong impression is that this part of the online world clubs together in networks to exchange information with like-minded people. The internet is in danger of becoming an enormous exercise in preaching to the converted.*

Helen Margetts picked up on this theme in her 2008 essay *Citizens and Consumers: Government Online versus Information for Informed Citizenship:*[207]

> *Some commentators have argued that this characteristic of internet behaviour allows people to customise their news, local information and political world to a quite alarming extent, so that they narrow their horizons, filter out any undesirable information and strengthen pre-existing judgements. Sunstein[208] argues that for citizens, the new plurality of information sources will lead to a read over of consumer sovereignty into news consumption: the creation of 'the Daily Me'.[209] In Sunstein's view, this fragmentation into individual views will lead to considerable difficulty in mutual understanding, as the internet increases people's ability to hear echoes of their own voices and works against the chance of any kind of shared public forum that signifies a democratic environment.*

As a remedy to this potential narrowing of horizons, Margetts points to the contribution that can be made by websites under public subsidy, with a mission to promote education and attention to public issues. She draws on the BBC site, noting its massive usage figures (around 12 million weekly unique visitors when she was writing in 2008, rising to 20.5 million weekly unique visitors in 2010[210]):

---

[206] http://www.bbc.co.uk/blogs/theeditors/2006/11/the_future_of_news.html.
[207] http://reutersinstitute.politics.ox.ac.uk/uploads/media/The_Price_of_Plurality_01.pdf.
[208] C. Sunstein, *Republic 2.0* (Princeton: Princeton University Press, 2007).
[209] N. Negroponte, *Being Digital* (New York: Knopf, 1995) and Sunstein, *Republic 2.0.*
[210] http://www.ukom.uk.net/news/?p=30.

By entering any part of the BBC website, users enter a much larger world regardless of their own steps to personalise their environment, by searching and bookmarking their favourite programs. They are offered links and reminders of government, politics and the public world, with the potential to take people outside the 'Daily Me'. In this way, the internet has the capacity to present citizens with a very large – as well as many very small – world.

With the BBC ranking fifth in the most popular web brands accessed by UK consumers in 2011[211] (after Google, MSN, Facebook, and Yahoo), its particular ability to contribute to this aspect of the public space is considerable. Chapter 10 below proposes a regulatory framework that applies consistent regulation across the broadcast, video on demand, and online provision of all providers with public service obligations.

---

[211] http://www.nielsen.com/uk/en/insights/press-room/2011-news/media_and_information-sites-thrive.html.

The Consumer Perspective

Given the wide disparity in regulation between and within different media platforms, identified above, questions arise of consumer confidence, and trust, in currently regulated and currently unregulated content. Recent research, some of which has been referred to in the preceding chapters, provides insights into consumer expectations, perceptions, and areas of confusion.

7.1. Digital consumption

Ofcom's *Communications Market Report,* published in August 2010,[212] included a look at what it called the 'Consumer's digital day'. It analysed how consumers use television, radio, broadband, and telephone services. The research identified the continuing popularity of television in the face of newer media platforms and devices, but also demonstrated significant generational divides: 'Two-thirds (67%) of media and communications activity conducted by people over 55 is carried out through a TV set or radio set.' For 16–24 year olds the figure was just over 30%:

> By contrast, among 16-24s, well over half (58%) their media and communications time is undertaken on a computer, mobile phone, or other handheld device ... compared to 18% for people aged over 55.

Overall, consumption of 'the more established devices and media, such as TV sets, radio sets, and print, generally increased with age'.

The research pointed to the key role of the television set:

> Video viewing was the most popular communications activity among consumers. It accounted for 212 minutes, or 40%, of all media and communications use in the day, with television viewed on a TV set (whether live, recorded or on-demand) representing 38 percentage points of that total (94% of all video viewing).

The generational divide was again significant in relation to video viewing:

> People aged 16–24 had a different media consumption profile. Only 26% of 16–24s' media time was spent watching television on a TV set, compared to the average of 38%. While watching video on devices other than TV sets remains a niche activity overall, it was more widespread among 16–24 year

---

[212] http://stakeholders.ofcom.org.uk/binaries/research/cmr/753567/CMR_2010_FINAL.pdf and http://stakeholders.ofcom.org.uk/binaries/research/811898/consumers-digital-day.pdf (Dec. 2010). See also http://stakeholders.ofcom.org.uk/binaries/research/cmr/cmr11/UK_CMR_2011_FINAL.pdf.

olds. Nineteen per cent of their video viewing (or 6% of their total media time) was through a device other than a TV set, compared with 7% among adults as a whole.

The average person was found to spend 252 minutes per week watching non-linear (on demand) audiovisual content across a variety of platforms and devices (17% of all viewing). Again there was a significant difference between consumption by the oldest and youngest. Average non-linear viewing was highest among 16–24s (26% of all viewing) and lowest among those aged 55+ (10%).

In addition to the proportion of time spent on different forms of digital media, the research also looked at attention levels and identified the potentially greater impact of on demand viewing on consumers. Downloaded TV and TV on demand delivered via a computer were found to attract amongst the highest levels of attention, while watching scheduled television attracted a lower average attention score than most media activities.

The research also noted the continuing growth in the popularity of BBC iPlayer:

Data from the BBC show that the total number of requests to view TV streams on iPlayer almost doubled from 53 million to 93 million in the 12 months to April 2010, a growth rate of 77%. While a small proportion of TV streams (8% in April 2010) consist of 'live' streams of programmes, the great majority (92% in April 2010) are video on demand streams.

7.2. Consumer assumptions about video on demand regulation

In December 2009 Ofcom published a qualitative research report prepared for it on video on demand. *The Regulation of Video-On-Demand: Consumer Views on What Makes Audiovisual Services 'TV-Like'*[213] was commissioned to inform implementation of the EU AVMS Directive under which regulation was extended to 'certain types of on-demand audiovisual services which are television-like'. The study looked at VOD services on TV and online platforms, including mobile devices, and was commissioned in order to 'gain an understanding of what consumers consider to be "TV-like" material and what their expectations are in terms of the key characteristics of such material'. However, the research provides broader insights into viewers' expectations and understanding (or lack of understanding) in relation to the regulation of video on demand.

By way of background the research noted that:

The traditional TV viewing experience was widely associated with ease, passivity and familiarity. The most common viewing context was watching TV programmes via a traditional TV screen in the living room, from the comfort of the sofa. This was the scenario most participants had grown up with, although it was recognised that viewing behaviour was increasingly changing over time due to multiple screen households and the rise of internet-based programme services ... Participants thought that TV represented societal shared values and reflected generally acceptable behaviour. TV was felt to provide news and information, offer entertainment and keep people in touch with the wider world. It was also a comforting presence in the household, frequently being switched on even when no one was watching.

---

[213] http://stakeholders.ofcom.org.uk/binaries/research/tv-research/vod.pdf.

TV navigation was associated with a sense of safety, signposting, and structure. Virgin Media's video on demand provision was also associated with these characteristics 'because of its clear menu presentation and well-signposted content sections'. The online environment was not generally associated with safety, signposting, and structure.

In relation to video on demand, it was generally regarded as 'simply another option for managing TV viewing', i.e. it was perceived as a means to time-shift content and tailor viewing to personal schedules, though the term 'video on demand' was not widely used in participants' day-to-day lives. The report observed that:

> *This was not merely a semantic issue; video on demand as a concept was not necessarily something that was regarded as distinct in its nature from other means of timeshifting, such as PVR recording, or services such as Sky Box Office. This was particularly true among those solely using TV VOD via Virgin Media; accessing VOD content via a TV platform heightened the perceived similarity between VOD and other forms of TV time-shifting. For most of these participants VOD was simply another way to access TV content: 'It's shows when you want them – simple as that.' Cardiff, 25-39yrs, heavy VOD [user].*
>
> *Among those who were familiar with the concept, VOD was firmly associated with the major UK broadcasters. There was a tendency to think of VOD services as primarily limited to TV services (among Virgin Media customers) and the main online broadcast catch-up services, such as BBC iPlayer, ITV Player, 4oD and Demand Five. Few participants were familiar with other services such as Joost, and these tended to be among the 18–24 year old heavy VOD users.*

The findings in relation to regulation were particularly significant:

> *It was broadly expected that all content which had previously been broadcast via a linear TV service would be regulated, even if accessed via an online catch-up service, such as BBC iPlayer. Most participants were not aware that broadcaster online catch-up services could show content that had not already been broadcast. Taking this into account, there was a general assumption that all content on such services was already subject to regulation.*

Interestingly, although participants valued the 'safety, signposting and structure' of the Virgin Media menu guide and there was clear evidence of concern across groups about the nature of online video content, there were also positive views towards the difference in regulation between television and the internet. The researchers identified 'a widely-held view that one of the things people value most about the internet is precisely its freedom, its lack of boundaries and – to an extent – the requirement to self-regulate one's behaviour when navigating it'.

A small number of individuals expressed concerns over the blurring of boundaries between broadcasting and the internet. Familiarity with the television set, and associations with safety with which it was imbued by these participants, led to unease over convergence:

> *The concerns of these individuals tended to centre around the protection of their children. The idea of internet video content being available through the previously 'safe' platform of the family TV screen felt intuitively uncomfortable; an invasion of a designated household safety zone. Their view was that if this was indeed to be the future of television, then all video content would need to be regulated to the same standards currently in place through the TV Broadcasting Code: 'I can't see why standards should change just because it is not scheduled viewing – why wouldn't it be regulated in the same way?' Belfast, 25–39yrs, light VOD.*

It is the comfort and safety associated with the television that makes the democratic imperative for transparency crucial for consumers. Without it, as we have seen, regulated and unregulated services will sit side by side and indistinguishable; brand associations will provide limited clues as to trustworthiness; and the credibility of journalism, and the wider media within which it sits, is put in jeopardy.

More broadly, the research identified an almost universal consensus across the research groups that 'some degree of protection' was necessary in a converged media landscape:

> *Main concerns surrounded the protection of children, and especially teenagers ... teenagers were felt to be a particularly vulnerable group, being naturally inclined to seek out illicit content, but not necessarily having the maturity to be emotionally prepared for what they might unearth.*

Concern for protection of children, as distinct from choices made by adults, is also demonstrated in research prepared for Ofcom on *Attitudes towards Sexual Material on Television.*[214] Although concerned with sexual and adult content rather than journalism, it usefully demonstrates a general distinction made between adults being enabled to make informed choices, and protection required for young children stumbling across, or older children actively seeking out, inappropriate material:

> *Protection of under-eighteens was seen as the main issue for all participants. The need to protect under-eighteens from sexual material was spontaneously raised in all discussion sessions by both parents and non-parents – although this concern was greater among parents. Children were the group that were seen as at risk from harm caused by exposure to sexual material, while many participants said adults could simply switch off if they were offended by what they saw ... Personal offence was less of a concern than protection of under-eighteens for most participants in most instances. The main reason for this was the belief that adults could make an informed choice themselves.*

Chapter 10 proposes a model of regulation that extends this distinction across media content: enabling adults and protecting children. It is also useful to note that participants in both these pieces of Ofcom research concluded that regulatory responsibility was shared between regulators, providers, and consumers. Participants in the research on video on demand saw the solution to converged regulation as:

> *a complex mix of independent and self-regulation, combined with parental and personal responsibility. It was felt that no single body could ultimately take sole responsibility.*[215]

---

[214] http://stakeholders.ofcom.org.uk/binaries/consultations/bcode09/annexes/sextv.pdf.
[215] http://stakeholders.ofcom.org.uk/binaries/research/tv-research/vod.pdf.

7.3. Sources of trusted news

New News Future News consumer research conducted for Ofcom in 2006[216] compared attitudes, where possible, to research carried out in 2002 for the ITV/BSC report *New News Old News.*[217] It asked questions about news sources 'ever' used: 94% of people said they used television as a news source at some time, similar to the 91% in 2002. Reported use of the internet 'ever' being used as a source for news had nearly doubled, from 15% to 27%. Among 16–24 year olds, use of television, radio, and newspapers as a source 'ever' used for news declined between 2002 and 2006, while use of the internet rose from 26% to 35%. As a main source of news television remained at 65% between 2002 and 2006, newspapers at around 15%, and the internet rose from 2% in 2002 to 6% in 2006.

Each year Ofcom's Media Tracker[218] asks questions of adults (aged 15+) who have a working television in their homes. The 2010 Tracker survey found that television was mentioned by 75% of respondents as being their main source of world news and by 49% as being their main source of local news. The internet was the second most-mentioned main source of world news (9%) while newspapers were the second most mentioned as the main source of local news (22%).

The research threw up interesting generational differences behind these broad figures. When asked about their main source of world news, younger respondents (15–24) were less likely than the other age groups to name television (67%), particularly when compared to the 45+ age group (81%). Respondents from the 15–24 age group were also more likely to name the internet (18%) as a source of world news, compared to 12% of 25–44s and 3% of the 45+ group. Besides television, those in the 45+ age group were more likely to mention radio (7%) compared to the 25–44s and 15–24s (5% and 1% respectively). Since 2005 newspapers saw a decline in the proportions of respondents naming them as their main source of either local or international news.

In relation to these bald figures 'the internet' is not further examined, nor are online and print newspapers differentiated, and so they do not provide insights into the type of websites and providers those aged 15–24 are using and therefore whether (as would be the case with, for example, the BBC's website) they would be subject to regulation. However, with 18% of younger people naming the internet as a source of world news compared with 3% of the 45+ group, a clear generational divide was identified by the research.

Ofcom's 2007 communications market special report *Ethnic Minority Groups and Communications Services*[219] found that people from ethnic minority groups (EMG) watched less television overall and much less BBC and ITV1 than the general population. The report said

> *a greater proportion of their viewing time is spent watching non-terrestrial channels, compared to the general population. Among all UK individuals, PSB [public service broadcasting] terrestrial channels account for over two-thirds of viewing, while this drops to just under half for EMG individuals.*

This is significant in understanding the impact that smaller, non-mainstream channels may have on the particular communities they serve, and therefore the impact that reduced regulation might have on those communities.

---

[216] http://stakeholders.ofcom.org.uk/binaries/research/tv-research/newnewsannexes.pdf.
[217] http://www.cardiff.ac.uk/jomec/resources/news.pdf.
[218] http://stakeholders.ofcom.org.uk/binaries/broadcast/reviews-investigations/psb-review/psb2010/Perceptions.pdf.
[219] http://stakeholders.ofcom.org.uk/binaries/research/cmr/ethnic_grps.pdf.

7.4. Attitudes to impartiality

On the issue of impartiality the research for *New News Future News* in 2006 found that 87% of respondents considered that impartiality on television and radio was important, with signs of a decrease since 2002 (when the figure was 97%). This fall was particularly true amongst 16 to 24 year olds: 93% considered impartiality important in 2002, down to 73% in 2006.

The Ofcom Media Tracker 2010 also asked questions about whether impartiality in news programming was important. Respondents were read out the following paragraph:

> *When talking about the news, impartiality means that each side is reported with equal weight, and that the organisation doing the reporting is not allowed to express their views on the merit of each side of the case. In the UK, television and radio channels are required by law to be impartial. Newspapers and the internet, while still having to be accurate, do not need to be impartial. How important do you personally think it is that news in general is impartial?*

Almost two-thirds of respondents (63%) felt that it was 'very important' and a further 28% felt it was important. Respondents were also asked about the importance of impartiality within specific areas of the media. Impartiality of television news was considered important almost universally (93%) and this was followed by radio (89%).

Richard Tait found similar support for broadcasting impartiality from a 2006 study[220] which analysed the Iraq War. It found 'overwhelming support (92%) for the idea that broadcasters should remain impartial and objective during wartime'.

However, while these levels of support for impartiality are undoubtedly high, using them to conclusively support impartiality in broadcasting is less than straightforward. The Ofcom Media Tracker 2010 found that support for the importance of impartiality also extended to newspapers (88%) and the internet (79%), neither of which have impartiality requirements imposed on them, indeed both of which are also valued for their opinion-driven partiality. In addition, *New News Future News* research in 2006 found that *perceived* levels of impartiality were significantly lower for the main terrestrial television news providers than they were in 2002.

> *In 2006, BBC One was seen as impartial by 54% of the sample (compared to 77% in 2002), and ITV1 by 41%, a decrease from 60% in 2002. One in five people (19%) felt that Channel 4's output was impartial in 2006, compared with 44% in 2002.*

The internet was considered to provide impartial news coverage by 11% of the sample, compared with 13% in 2002. Levels of trust in terrestrial television news outlets were also shown to have diminished since 2002, while trust in the internet to tell the truth about the news rose (22% to 29%).

However, the report noted that the extent to which people feel the news is impartial or trustworthy is dependent on the type of 'granularity' of the question asked. When respondents were asked about the individual news programmes they have watched, much higher proportions of people said that the programmes were impartial and trustworthy.

---

[220] J. Lewis, R. Brookes, N. Mosdell, and T. Threadgold, *Shoot First and Ask Questions Later* (2006).

It concluded that:

> *The difference in response between 2002 and 2006 points to a climate or attitude towards news provision which is arguably more sceptical – or realistic – about news sources and their ability to be impartial.*

IPSOS/MORI consumer research[221] for the BBC 2007 report *From Seesaw to Wagon Wheel*[222] found that:

> *Whilst 44% of those surveyed think that it is impossible for broadcasters to be impartial, the majority (84%) do agree that although it may be difficult to achieve, broadcasters must try very hard give the public a fair and informed view on events and issues.*

In addition, it noted the scepticism, or realism, about broadcasters' ability to achieve impartiality identified in the *New News Future News* research: '61% think that although broadcasters may think they give a fair and informed view, a lot of the time they don't.'

A further question in Ofcom's Media Tracker 2010 also asked respondents which, if any, sources they trusted and felt presented fair and unbiased world news coverage.

> *Overall, more respondents felt that television gave a fairer and more unbiased source of world news coverage than any other medium, mentioned by 72% of respondents overall. However, those in the oldest age group (45+) were more likely to mention television than the youngest age group (15–24) – 74% and 67% respectively. The internet was the second most-mentioned – by 7% of all respondents.*

Again a clear generational divide emerged in relation to trusting the internet: younger respondents (15–24s) were more likely to choose the internet (13%) compared with 4% of those aged 45+. Taken together with the earlier figures demonstrating 18% of younger respondents naming the internet as a source of world news, use of and trust in the internet appear to be associated, although again whether the trusted internet sources were regulated is not explored.

7.5. Generational divides and consumer preferences

Television has, until recently, been identified by the public as the media device they would 'most miss'. However, Ofcom's adult and children's media literacy reports (based on surveys of over 4,000 adults and children) were published in April 2011.[223] For the first time, the reports found that 16–24 year olds did not say they would miss television the most, instead they were more likely to say their mobile phones (28%) or the internet (26%) ahead of television (23%). And among children aged 12–15 the same pattern emerged, with most mentioning mobiles as most missed (26%), and the internet and television level (24%). While television remained the medium that would be missed the most for the UK as a whole, it was found to have decreased from 50% in 2009 to 44% in 2010.

---

[221] http://www.bbc.co.uk/bbctrust/assets/files/pdf/review_report_research/impartiality_21century/c_quantitative_research.pdf.

[222] http://www.bbc.co.uk/bbctrust/assets/files/pdf/review_report_research/impartiality_21century/report.pdf.

[223] http://media.ofcom.org.uk/2011/04/19/half-of-parents-say-they-know-less-about-the-internet-than-their-children. See also http://stakeholders.ofcom.org.uk/binaries/research/cmr/cmr11/UK_CMR_2011_FINAL.pdf.

I do not underestimate the significant role of television, and related comprehensive regulation that has been attached to it, but the recommendations in Chapter 10 are mindful of the clear emerging generational divide reflected in consumer research, and the emerging importance of video on demand and online audiovisual content to print and broadcast providers alike.

8. Conclusions on Regulatory Challenges

The chief conclusion from the exploration of regulatory requirements in Chapters 2 to 6 above, and underpinned by consumer attitudes reviewed in Chapter 7, is that current regulation is failing to address the democratic value in 'enabling' the citizen to navigate, and engage with, the range of content across the public space. It is failing to support informed choices about content: be it partial or impartial; regulated or unregulated; public service or purely commercial; and whether derived from broadcasting, print, video on demand, or online.

The 'protection' provided for consumers of all television and radio services could be argued to set a benchmark for standards across the rest of the media, but this position fails to acknowledge the interconnected media landscape with which citizens, and particularly younger citizens, proactively engage. Meanwhile freedom of the press is linked to self-regulation but the tensions between the values and aspirations of the broadsheet and red-top ends of the press, intensified by competition in emerging online markets, call into question the traditional notions of the press itself. The regulation of video on demand content is currently masked by related broadcasting standards, but the reality is a minimal set of rules disconnected from audience assumptions and expectations.

The challenge arising from these inconsistencies of approach is to consider the role of the public space that exists across the media, in our democratic life, and the role of regulation in supporting that public space. Regulation can provide a required baseline on which consumer expectations in relation to, for example, a right of reply or a prohibition on incitement to hatred can rest. It can also demonstrate the aspirations of a provider, voluntarily undertaken: their ethical values and recognition of responsibilities, linked to sanctions for failure. Regulated and unregulated material will inevitably sit side by side but without transparency consumers cannot distinguish between it, and make informed choices about the weight to give information and the trust to place in different providers. And providers themselves cannot market their offerings accordingly, nor, without an open, flexible, and credible framework, can new providers choose to access the accreditation and public confidence that regulation can confer.

A number of particular regulatory challenges have been identified so far and they are summarised immediately below. Chapter 9 seeks to identify proposals on how to address them, and Chapter 10 concludes with recommendations on a new settlement for media content, consumers, providers, and regulators.

8.1. Regulation is out of step with convergence

- As audiovisual content (whether originating from broadcasting, print, video on demand, or other online providers) converges, there is a blurring of content boundaries and regulatory responsibilities. Duplication, conflict, and obfuscation are already emerging within the current system. The advent of internet-connected televisions can only serve to accentuate the potential for consumers' confusion over whether the content with which they engage is regulated and, if so, to what extent and by whom. Without clarity and consistency consumers cannot make informed choices, both for themselves and in relation to children.
- The converging of media across a variety of platforms exposes how far practical considerations have determined, and justified, the differing requirements imposed: for example, between broadcasting and newspapers, and between scheduled and on demand content. Where we can regulate we do, where we cannot we do not, and the narrative we tell about 'push' and 'pull' media has been used to justify these practical considerations. However, as consumers make active selections across a range of broadcast media, including the hundreds of digital channels, and newspapers are readily available online, such narratives become less helpful. The European AVMS Directive imposes a set of basic editorial and commercial demands on both television and video on demand services. However, the decision to impose gold-plated comprehensive rules on scheduled television, and place no additional regulation on video on demand services, has been a matter of statutory choice.

8.2. Regulation is Out of Step with Public Expectations, Understanding and Requirements

- Regulatory confusion risks a breakdown in public trust across the platforms as comprehensively regulated, lightly regulated, and unregulated content increasingly sits side by side. There is already confusion over who regulates what, who deals with complaints, and where consumer expectations should lie in relation to material provided on different platforms.
- The internet is understood by consumers to be unregulated and yet the size of the BBC's online presence throws even that assumption into doubt; clarity is required over where online regulation begins and ends, and where public service regulation begins and ends.
- Consumers' assumptions around video on demand are not met by the limited regulation that applies, and informal self-regulation by mainstream players is masking the difference in regulatory standards between scheduled and video on demand provision. In addition, consumer familiarity with mainstream brands does not apply either to new providers, or for younger, converged consumers.
- Impartiality has been at the heart of broadcasting, partiality at the heart of newspaper freedom. As the two media converge this distinction begins to appear arbitrary. Consumers see impartiality as a worthy aspiration but express this view for print and the internet (where there is no such requirement) as well as for broadcasting. Even where it is a requirement, for broadcasting, consumers do not

always perceive it as being achieved. Indeed impartiality requirements are already inconsistent. They are pragmatically waived in relation to some international content; limited to the political and/or industrial arena for most broadcast media; but significantly extended as requirements for the BBC. All of which leads to the potential for confused consumer expectations and decline in regulatory credibility. Clarity over the value, purpose, and place of impartiality is required.

- The attitudes and media consumption of consumers who are younger, or from minority ethnic groups, contrast with those of general audiences and need to be accounted for as media regulation is developed. Younger, converged, consumers do not have the same reference points that assist older consumers in forming expectations around different content, and differing regulation is likely to appear increasingly arbitrary and ineffectual. Meanwhile, services providing for diverse communities are challenging notions of impartiality and generally accepted standards.
- 'Adequate protection' of the public is the starting point for the 2003 Communications Act's approach to standards regulation but does this remain the right starting point? Protection may have been possible when it was first enshrined in the 1954 Television Act but is protection in relation to adults now meaningful? What are the limitations on protection when sources of content are unlimited (given the wider online content world)? And how desirable is protection of adults as a goal? Arguably, singling out broadcast content for comprehensive regulation gives a false sense of regulatory security, and leaves the consumer exposed and unprepared for the limited regulation of video on demand content, self-regulation of newspapers, and the unregulated online world. This is particularly significant when the content derived from each may be indistinguishable and delivered via a television set associated by consumers with signposting, structure, and safety.
- Meanwhile, protection of children, identified as a key area of consumer concern, is blurred with protection of adults in relation to broadcasting, yet is not delivered in a meaningful way in relation to the rules on video on demand material.

8.3. Regulation is Out of Step with Provider Understanding, Expectations and Requirements

- As broadcasters provide text-based articles on their websites and newspapers provide audio and video content on theirs, how far does regulation based on assumptions about air waves and print have a future? Is the means of distribution important, or the nature and purpose of the content and the values and credibility of its provider?
- As the BBC widens the regulatory standards gap between itself and other broadcasters, we may wish to consider how far comprehensive standards obligations should be narrowed to those providers with public service commitments; how far commercial broadcasters without such commitments should be subject to different regulation; and ways in which a tiered approach to regulation could incentivise providers to ensure that such moves enrich rather than erode public debate.

- Reputational risks to regulators and providers are emerging over areas of duplication (between the BBC Trust and Ofcom), of tension (between ATVOD and PCC members), and confusion (the extraordinary range of complaint-handling responsibilities across different bodies).
- Opportunities to support voluntary regulation by content providers are being missed. The PCC Code has offered membership to online providers, including bloggers, but even prior to 'hackgate' was seen by many as discredited. The self-regulatory code to which video on demand providers adhered was dismantled with the advent of ATVOD. Voluntary adherence to the Ofcom Broadcasting Code is being informally adopted by some video on demand providers but lacks transparency; meanwhile, regulation under the Ofcom Code cannot be offered to wider providers (beyond Ofcom licensees) under the existing statutory framework.

8.4. Regulatory Leverage is Shifting

- Social and economic imperatives, but also pragmatic approaches, have always underpinned regulation, i.e. regulation is imposed where there is leverage. For broadcasting, analogue spectrum leverage is receding and digital spectrum leverage is limited. Consideration of the purpose and practice of regulation across platforms is required.
- Occupation of the regulated space will need to be incentivised to prevent migration to unregulated platforms and to ensure compliance. Statutory regulation has also traditionally been linked to the power of the audiovisual medium and its potential to influence hearts and minds, and yet such considerations are not applied to video on demand services.
- Regulatory leverage is also shifting for print media. The press has strenuously resisted the possibility of state regulation over decades. However, with Northern and Shell titles operating with impunity outside the PCC's authority, widening differences in the offerings from the quality and red-top ends of the market, and competition for authority from ATVOD, the future of the current regulatory framework was in doubt well before the most recent developments in the phone-hacking scandal.

9. A Decade of Debate and Observations for the Next Decade

The regulatory challenges identified in Chapters 2 to 8 have been stealing up on us for some time. A range of key papers and speeches over the past decade have surfaced a variety of recommendations in response. These are reviewed below, and followed by a range of contributions provided by regulators, practitioners, and academics interviewed for this paper, providing a useful background to the recommendations set out in Chapter 10.

9.1. Limiting impartiality requirements

Nearly ten years ago, the then broadcasting regulators (the ITC and BSC) commissioned the research publication *New News, Old News*.[224] This responded to concerns about disengagement amongst sections of the democratic community, in particular the young and members of minority ethnic groups, from news programming. Authors Ian Hargreaves and James Thomas made key recommendations on relaxing the rules on impartiality for non-mainstream channels, and providing transparency for internet users.

First, in relation to impartiality, the report argued that:

> *It may be that a more opinionated style of broadcast news, originated from well outside the UK broadcasting mainstream, is helpful in the overall news mix, so long as consumers are aware what they are getting and which services conform to impartiality rules and which do not. The time has come when a range of experimentation should be encouraged.*
>
> *However, the clear primary thrust of the evidence we have gathered is that there is also very strong public support for the existing regime of broadcasting impartiality, which points to a cautious approach. The most sensible course is to create an opening for OFCOM to recommend to the Secretary of State variation in the impartiality rules, where the channels involved are of minority interest and where they do not threaten the central, impartial reputation of mainstream UK television news. The principle should be both to regulate and to encourage broadcasters to innovate.*

It clarified its view that:

> *Any channel granted such exemption would still be required to conform to any general requirement of British law, such as statutes forbidding incitement to racial hatred, or to secure the protection of children.*

[224] http://www.cardiff.ac.uk/jomec/resources/news.pdf.

Secondly, in relation to transparency for internet users, the report concluded:

> There is certainly no case to be made for applying content regulation of the type deployed in broadcasting to the world wide web as a whole, even if this were possible. However, the internet is a medium which will no doubt benefit over time if users are able to show discrimination over the types of information they receive, screening out what they consider distasteful or unreliable.

It recommended that Ofcom 'be charged with a responsibility to respond to established public demand for a regulated, public service dimension to internet-based services. This might include kite-marked sites, search engines and filtering systems.' It argued that such mechanisms would 'respond to sustained public demand for reassurance about standards on the internet. It should, however, also be made clear that those who want a wholly unregulated experience of the internet subject only to the constraints of the criminal law are entitled to have that.'[225]

The approach proposed in Chapter 10 below seeks to build on, and extend, both these 2002 recommendations. *New News Old News* recommended a broad requirement of impartiality for most broadcast content, and allowing minority channels to opt out of this regulation. It separately argued for transparency over internet provision, acknowledged demand for a public service dimension to online services and recommended regulation, combined with kite-marking, to enable the public to distinguish this content. However, the blurring of boundaries between sources of content, most starkly illustrated by internet-connected television, has moved the debate on. I argue for a combination of both these recommendations: provision of impartial and partial content across media platforms, clearly distinguishable through associated standards marks, with impartiality linked to public service commitments. Under this approach the public would be enabled in discriminating between content that conforms to different regulatory requirements, and commercial providers would be enabled to 'opt in' to the tier of regulation that best serves to differentiate their offering.

9.2. Protecting or enabling the consumer?

In 2009 James Murdoch was invited to give the prestigious annual MacTaggart Lecture. Presciently entitled 'The Absence of Trust',[226] his lecture decried 'analogue attitudes in a digital age', a policy framework built on spectrum scarcity, and a belief in 'omniscient authority' and the 'wisdom and activity of governments and regulators' who refuse to trust the people who matter: 'the people who pay the bills as customers and as tax-payers'. He spoke of the unacknowledged partiality implicit in the very selection of news stories and said the effect of the current system 'is not to curb bias – bias is present in all news media – but simply to disguise it':

> The greatest divergence between the rest of the media and broadcasting is the unspoken approach to the customer. In the regulated world of Public Service Broadcasting the customer does not exist: he or she is a passive creature – a viewer – in need of protection. In other parts of the media world – including pay television and newspapers – the customer is just that:

[225] These ideas were further developed in the 2007 Ofcom report *New News, Future News* (http://stakeholders.ofcom.org.uk/market-data-research/tv-research/newnews) and the 2008 RISJ publication *The Price of Plurality*: http://reutersinstitute.politics.ox.ac.uk/uploads/media/The_Price_of_Plurality_01.pdf.
[226] http://www.mgeitf.co.uk/uploads/pdf/MurdochLecture.pdf.

someone whose very freedom to choose makes them important. And because they have power they are treated with great seriousness and respect, as people who are perfectly capable of making informed judgements about what to buy, read, and go and see.

He sought to debunk the argument that switching on a television is less of an active choice than buying a newspaper when he referred to the deliberate act of consumption and argued for independence from regulatory supervision and dependency:

Independence is sustained by true accountability – the accountability owed to customers. People who buy the newspapers, open the application, decide to take out the television subscription – people who deliberately and willingly choose a service which they value.

Murdoch argued that genuine independence in the news media is guaranteed not by 'committees, regulators, trusts of advisory bodies' but by 'profit'.

Here I argue for a positive role for regulation – relevant to consumers, providers, and participants – as part of a mixed, tiered offering set out in Chapter 10 below. Notwithstanding criminal phone-hacking developments, Murdoch's jibe that the regulated world treats the customer as a 'passive creature ... in need of protection' is instructive. I propose an approach that safeguards protection for children, but limits notions of protection to the vulnerable, and seeks to enable the public to navigate media content as informed adult citizens, making active choices.

9.3. Calling time on analogue regulation

In his 2010 RTS Fleming Memorial Lecture 'Calling Time on Analogue Regulation – an Agenda for the Next Communications Act',[227] Professor Stewart Purvis noted that while '92.7% of households in the UK already have some form of digital television', the final switchover from analogue transmitters to digital terrestrial television will be symbolic: 'It will be the moment at which calibrating regulation by access to transmitters passes its sell-by date. That's because technology now allows so many more players to reach audiences within spectrum and without spectrum.'

Musing on the confluence of new and old media Purvis said:

While I wrote this lecture in my study at home there were three pieces of technology on my desk. On my computer I can visit livestation.com to watch TV news being streamed live from both regulated and unregulated providers around the world. On my internet radio I can browse the list of hundreds of stations. I have absolutely no idea whether they are radio stations licensed in their own country or coming from the front room of an unlicensed enthusiast via the internet. I can also select from unregulated podcasts from home and abroad. On my phone I have an app that cost me 59p that allows me to listen to 200 stations from Australia – most of them licensed by the Australian equivalent of Ofcom, but some not. If it is deemed that as a listener I need regulatory protection from potential harm and offence caused by licensed stations in the UK, how come I don't need similar protection from unlicensed stations from around the world?

---

[227] http://www.rts.org.uk/sites/default/files/Fleming_Lecture_text_2010_Stewart_Purvis_CBE.pdf.

His proposal was to 'focus on where statutory powers are really needed, and create a flexible framework to allow the rest to move over time to self-regulation'.

The statutory powers Purvis identified as essential were:

> *that broadcasters put their licences at risk if they break the laws of the land on incitement to crime or racial hatred or commit other criminal offences. Over and above that the primary area which I would reserve for statutory powers is the protection of children.*

He argued that 'Complaints about lesser "harm and offence" and about fairness and privacy from viewers caught up in programmes could be handled by a self-regulatory body.'

Purvis made a distinction between '"public broadcasters" on the one hand and "private broadcasters" on the other' and argued that the next Communications Act should make the regulatory requirements proportionate. He continued: 'Bearing in mind that much of what the BBC and Channel Four already produce is online we should really be talking about "publicly-owned media", "privately-owned media" and not forgetting "community media" of the kind pioneered by community radio stations' and concluded:

> *And always have in mind that one day there may be no such thing as 'television', 'radio' and 'online', just audio and visual content, some live, some recorded, which you select using apps on your phone as well as buttons on your TV handset, literally thousands of content offerings, all jostling for attention on a screen near you.*

The distinction between public and private media is a useful one. It provides clarity in distinguishing why certain providers (the BBC, Channel 4, and S4C) must be subject to statutory regulatory controls because of their defining public service identity. On the other hand some commercially owned providers (ITV and Channel 5) currently adhere to a range of public service obligations in return for certain benefits, notably, Purvis notes, a place on the PSB multiplexes (discussed in Chapter 1). Equally, related standards requirements could be part of this regulatory quid pro quo for as long as it remains in place.

Purvis also argued for a 'focus on where statutory powers are really needed' and the creation of a flexible framework that allows other providers 'to move over time to self-regulation'. In Chapter 10 below I argue that such flexibility could be achieved through statutory regulation for public media (including requirements for commercial public service providers), and incentivising private media to opt in to independent, voluntary regulation. The protection of children, and laws against incitement, to which Purvis referred would be built in to each tier.

9.4. Consistent protection for children across media

On 6 June 2011 Reg Bailey, Chief Executive of the Mothers' Union, concluded his independent review, commissioned by the Government, looking at 'the pressures on children to grow up too quickly',[228] and published his report of an Independent Review of the Commercialisation and Sexualisation of Childhood: *Letting Children be Children*.[229] The report was concerned with reducing the risks of the premature commercialisation and sexualisation of children, rather than with journalism or wider

---

[228] http://www.education.gov.uk/b0074315/bailey-review.
[229] https://www.education.gov.uk/publications/eOrderingDownload/Bailey%20Review.pdf.

content concerns. However, it is relevant to the issues around convergence raised here in that its survey of the views of over 1,500 parents, children and young people aged 7–16 and a further 1,000 parents interviewed online, and over 500 children and young people surveyed by the Office for the Children's Commissioner for England, identified opaque complaints systems and a sense of powerlessness among consumers, and informed conclusions in relation to the significance of media education.

In relation to broadcasting and video on demand services, the report noted particular concerns 'that the television programmes that people have traditionally watched as family viewing, such as talent shows and soaps, are starting to push the boundaries of acceptability by including increasingly sexualised content'. And that

> *serious concerns have been voiced to the Review about the ease of access to age-restricted and adult-only material on the internet and through video on demand and via mobile phones, and the inconsistent, and in some cases non-existent, controls on accessing such material by children and young people.*

The report called for the content of pre-watershed television programming to better meet parents' expectations and in relation to video on demand material it concluded that it should be made easier for parents to block adult and age-restricted material from the internet. The report wanted to see quality assurance for media and commercial literacy resources and education 'to help children develop their emotional resilience to the commercial and sexual pressures that today's world places on them'. It argued for independent evaluation of this provision not just to measure take-up 'but, crucially, to assess its effectiveness'. The report recognised the confusing variety of co-, self-, and statutory regulators across the media (also articulated by the House of Lords' Inquiry,[230] discussed in Chapter 3 above, whose findings in relation to complaints are found in Annex 2).

Bailey's review usefully prioritised protection of children, and the necessity for transparent and consistent labelling around age appropriateness, supported by an emphasis on filtering mechanisms and monitored media literacy resources. It also recognised the array of regulators that exist across the media, although it did not tackle the underlying differences between regulatory regimes as I seek to do in the proposals set out in Chapter 10. Its recommendations were grounded in the realities of current regulation rather than seeking to effect change in the overall regulatory framework.

However, perhaps the report's most significant contribution was to seek to place citizens and consumers back at the heart of the government's agenda. In contrast to the launch of the Government's communications review in May 2011 (see Chapter 1) which opened the debate within a context of economic growth, Bailey's report sought to position parents and children, together with their requirements and expectations of the public space, right at the centre of business and regulatory development. Likewise, my contention is that the starting point for the next Communications Act should be to place the citizen, and the democratic purposes of the public space provided across broadcast, print, video on demand, and online platforms, at the heart of regulatory and economic development.

---

[230] http://www.publications.parliament.uk/pa/ld201012/ldselect/ldcomuni/166/16602.htm.

9.5. Reforming the press within wider regulatory convergence

Speaking to the Royal Television Society in Cambridge in September 2011,[231] Jeremy Hunt acknowledged the democratic role of the media, marking it out from other industries:

> *Of course all sectors need competition to protect consumers and make sure they get the best deal. But other industries do not define our culture in the way the media does. A country's character, the unique bonds that define its society and its democratic institutions, are all shaped by its media. So we need to take special care to ensure we have vibrant, free – even raucous – debate. We need to ensure that there is the opportunity for multiple voices. And we must take care that power is never over-concentrated in a few hands.*

He also signalled a measured response to the phone-hacking scandal, and recognised the need for cross-platform regulation:

> *it is important that in our desire to address the issues surrounding phone-hacking, we do not over-compensate. Our free press has served us incredibly well. So we do not want any changes to result in the back door imposition of statutory broadcast-style regulation ... when it comes to a new regulatory framework for the newspaper industry we have an opportunity to look to the future. My challenge to you is this: work with us to establish a credible, independent regulatory framework which has the confidence of consumers and we will support it as the one-stop regulatory framework to be applied across all the technology platforms you operate. This won't replace traditional broadcast regulation. But for a newspaper industry moving to IPTV it could supersede it – giving Britain the prize of being the first country in the world where a new generation of innovative, cross-platform media companies are able to grow on the back of the world's first converged regulatory framework.*

The aim of Chapter 10 is to set out proposals for transition to a credible framework of standards regulation across platforms: a framework that recognises the traditions from which different media are derived, but provides a consistency and coherence across media platforms that the current arrangements lack. It is a framework that promotes the exercise of informed choice by consumers and commercial and ethical choices by providers, while protecting children and the vulnerable.

9.6. Lessons from a cross-media code

In addition to the proposals and debate set out above, a number of ideas and instructive lessons from overseas emerged from those I interviewed. These are set out as useful counterpoints and complementary contributions to the recommendations which follow.

Following the invitation by Jeremy Hunt (referred to above) to consider cross-media regulation, it is instructive to consider an attempt to match technological and content convergence with wholly converged, 'one-size-fits-all', regulation. In an interview Stephen Whittle explained his experience, early in 2011, of being involved in drawing up a cross-media Code for the Technology and Free Media Zone in Dubai that licences around 400 different international and Middle Eastern content providers, including Thomson

---

[231] http://www.culture.gov.uk/news/ministers_speeches/8428.aspx.

Reuters, News International, *Time Out Dubai*'s publisher ITP, the BBC and CNN, entertainment channels, providers of video games, and film studios. He explained: 'They were looking for a content code that would be applicable to all those different content providers which forces you to think a bit about what is the essence [of regulation], and what is not so important anymore.'[232] Overall he observed:

> *In that environment actually I came to the conclusion that impartiality was not as important as accuracy and fairness as a requirement, because there's no way that Reuters is suddenly going to give up on impartiality because that's what marks its brand. So was it really necessary to impose impartiality ... and then run the business risk of losing the people you hope to attract to your free media zone in the first place? We came to the conclusion that accuracy and fairness were more important than impartiality because people who were impartial, and prided themselves on their impartiality, were not going to suddenly walk away from it because they were not required to demonstrate it in Dubai.*

The proposed cross-media code therefore contained requirements for accuracy, fairness, and privacy, specifically requiring the separation of fact and comment in order for the consumer to be entirely clear in identifying material that is factual reporting, as opposed to material that is opinion.

Harm and offence, and protection of the under-18s, Whittle explained, were dealt with through a combination of cultural norms, information, and electronic protections:

> *There is no desire whatsoever for a watershed because people felt the entertainment channels were essentially protected in the sense that they're subscription channels. But also because everybody's sense of the unspoken rules in society meant that you did not need to write that in because people would know what would be commercially acceptable in the context in which they were operating. So you could argue that in a certain sense it's about a greater sense of provider responsibility, self-regulation in that sense.*

In Whittle's view there is no easy transition to a cross-media code for the UK given the disparities between the two cultures and markets. In Dubai, for example, newspapers that would fight the notion of licensing in the UK tooth and claw accept it as the price to be paid for operating in that market. As Whittle put it: 'You cut your principles according to the market in which you find yourself.' He also noted that while freedom of expression is enshrined in the constitution in Dubai there are limitations placed on it, both in terms of political debate and cultural values:

> *with the entertainment channels, they are going to be so careful because they know what the limits of toleration on their operations are likely to be when it comes to bare elbows or a kiss at any time of the day or night ... Not all of this translates very readily to the UK obviously because broadcasting regulation is culture bound. But it is interesting that it is possible to write a Code that provides essentially a baseline.*

The notion of a baseline for content standards is returned to in the proposals of Chapter 10 below as part of a tiered approach to regulation across platforms.

---

[232] Interview May 2009.

9.7. The impact of cultural expectations

The cultural context to which Whittle refers, and its role in informing media practice, is by no means limited to Dubai where the 'limits of toleration' are clearly understood. Nick Catliff, a managing director at independent production company Lion Televison, pointed to a web of commercial, brand, and cultural interests that he argued influence content as much, if not more, than regulation. Lion makes cross-platform programming for audiences in Europe, Asia, the UK, and US but, Catliff observed:[233] 'Global content is actually very, very hard to do.' What works for a Swedish audience, who may be relaxed about nudity, will not work for a French audience, he observed. A 'wife swap' format will work in Europe but may scandalise in India. In relation to accuracy, the brand will dictate the standards to be adhered to:

> We do a lot of programmes in the US where regulation is entirely different. You are largely dealing in a cable universe where it's all about profile and branding – it's about branding more than anything else. So being 'on brand' for the network, whether it's Discovery or TLC [The Learning Channel] or History is what really, really counts. It's a commercial imperative there, rather than regulatory issues, that really pushes you ... At National Geographic, effectively there's a regulatory regime within the network of fact-checking within that organisation, because they're owned by the National Geographic [Society]. National Geographic will fact check you to death because 'our brand is we get our facts right'; other people have different brand issues.

Catliff points to UK broadcasters adopting a similar approach, particularly the BBC in reaction to 'fakery' accusations over footage of from its programme *A Year with the Queen*: 'The end result of that is no one wants to be the person who is responsible for a screw up. It's not regulation; supervision would be the way to describe it.' Similarly, he suggests, a newspaper that 'rather pompously reinforces its brand on its complaints page' is not responding to regulatory requirements: 'that's not regulation, that's enlightened self interest'.

In addition to the cultural expectations of audiences, and the commercial imperatives of brands, Catliff noted the impact of public service values on his generation of programme makers who at some time have worked for, and been trained by, the BBC:

> For a company like Lion ... we're all broadly speaking BBC people even if we're not. That's the culture within which we all swim. To be completely honest we don't really notice regulation because we sucked it with our mother's milk, we know what is and isn't acceptable.

However, for the next generation of programme makers and audiences he detects a significant shift:

> The generation coming through see it very differently. We see 'that's the BBC, that's public service television, that's one set of rules, the rules are slightly different in the digital world, and they're different online'. If you haven't been brought up with that, you haven't seen these different generations of technology, and delivery platforms coming through, then in the end it's all pictures, it's all content ... so there's an absolute loss of geography and chronology there, which is really, really difficult.

[233] Interview May 2011.

Similarly he argued: 'web native [consumers] under 25 don't necessarily pick up on all the dog whistles' signalling different expectations for different content when it is all delivered in the same way. 'Young people, are themselves platform neutral, they won't know, can't tell the difference.'

The proposals in Chapter 10 argue for a transparency of content requirements, through a simple, tiered system of 'standards marks' that would replace reliance on 'dog whistles' and brand associations. In this way consumers, and indeed the next generation of programme makers, would not be required to have the understanding of historic broadcasting and newspaper regulation that, Catliff suggests, is currently essential in order to grasp the complexity of existing regulatory frameworks.

9.8. Broadcasting regulation where standards are a selling point

A number of those interviewed proposed a move away from comprehensive, statutory broadcasting regulation for all but publicly funded/public service organisations.

For Eve Salomon, author of the UNESCO/Commonwealth Broadcasting Association *Guidelines for Broadcasting Regulation,*[234] there are three issues on which she has found widespread acceptance across the globe: 'one is protecting children, one is an obligation for news to be truthful, and [thirdly] prohibitions against hate speech'. These, she argued, should provide the basis for formal regulation and, beyond that, 'there's huge scope for self-regulation'. Canadian Broadcasting, in Salomon's view, provided a useful model for voluntary regulation that could be extended across platforms. Under this model the Canadian Broadcast Standards Council[235] (CBSC), an independent, non-governmental, voluntary organisation created and funded by Canada's private broadcasters, administers standards established by its members (more than 730 private sector radio and television stations).

CBSC operates with the approval of the federal regulator (the Canadian Radio-television and Telecommunications Commission or CRTC) but is not a statutory body.[236] Complaints about any broadcasters who are not members of the CBSC (including public broadcasters) are dealt with by the CRTC, which also acts as an appeals panel on CBSC decisions. CBSC's adjudication panels are made up of members representing the public and the broadcast industry in equal numbers and can impose penalties for members who breach the required standards.

This model, Eve Salomon suggested, works because there are commercial incentives. There is a strong business case for these private enterprises to become and remain members, and to adhere to the standards they themselves establish and develop as societal trends emerge. Nearly all of Canada's private broadcasters are members but, as a voluntary organisation, its credibility is not undermined by a less than 100% membership rate. An added incentive for the industry to make the system work is the threat of a statutory alternative if their self-regulatory framework fails.

In the case of UK broadcasting, moves towards independent regulation would represent a significant deregulatory departure from the comprehensive statutory requirements currently imposed. Conversely, for video on demand providers, it could represent a levelling up from the basic rules already explored and a new consistency of approach.

Pete Johnson explained[237] that ATVOD would be supportive of such a move but under the current legislative framework it would have to be initiated by industry or government:

[234] http://unesdoc.unesco.org/images/0018/001832/183285e.pdf.
[235] http://www.ccnr.ca/english/index.php.
[236] http://www.cbsc.ca/english/documents/speeches/Notes%20for%20address%20_Trinidad(as%20delivered).pdf.
[237] Interview May 2011

Provided there is an appetite for that from industry, and also a means of funding that, ATVOD, philosophically, would be very supportive in playing a part in establishing additional protections for consumers. But it has to come from industry. The industry has to say 'Actually we think our consumers and our industry would benefit from greater protections than are provided by the [Audiovisual Media Services] Directive and the Communications Act, we would like to do something about that collectively and so let's work out a way of funding that'. Because all [ATVOD's] funding comes from fees charged under the statutory regime. And it would be inappropriate for us to divert those funds into a voluntary scheme.

So provided the will of industry is there, and the mechanism for funding the self-regulatory code, then ATVOD is philosophically pre-disposed to doing that ... They [additional requirements] could come from government as well, but with the next Communications Act not expected to be on the statute until 2015, one of the things that industry will want to consider in relation to the Communications Act is whether it is in their interests to establish greater self regulation or whether it is in their interests to simply rest on the current statutory regime and see whether or if that is supplemented through statute in 2015.

Eve Salomon saw positive examples where voluntary regulation has already begun in the UK, for example the set of 'Good Practice principles' adhered to by BT Vision[238] and others in relation to audiovisual content, as part of the Broadband Stakeholder Group.[239] These principles relate to the provision of information about audiovisual content that is commercially produced or acquired (they do not apply to user-generated content or advertising). They commit providers to promoting and enabling media literacy and offering content information in order to empower users and to allow them to make informed choices about the content 'that they and their families access/consume/watch'.[239] Providers may rely on the Ofcom Broadcasting Code, BBC Editorial Guidelines, and the British Board of Film Classification (BBFC) ratings to inform their decision-making about the provision of information as well as their own 'brand values'.

Salomon also pointed to related precedents in encouraging a range of organisations to coalesce in partnership around a common goal, as has been the case with the UK Council for Child Internet Safety (UKCCIS), which says it 'brings together over 170 organisations and individuals from government, industry, law enforcement, academia and charities, including parenting groups ... to work in partnership to keep children and young people safe online'.[241] Similarly, the Pan European Game Information (PEGI) replaced an array of national age rating systems with a single system now used in 30 countries in Europe, 'to help European parents make informed decisions on buying computer games'.[242]

[238] http://www.btplc.com/Thegroup/RegulatoryandPublicaffairs/Codeofpractice/Goodpracticeframework/Goodpractice-framework.htm.
[239] www.broadbanduk.org.
[240] http://www.audiovisualcontent.org/audiovisualcontent.pdf.
[241] http://www.education.gov.uk/ukccis.
[242] http://www.pegi.info/en/index/id/952.

9.9. Transparency and media awareness for an informed, engaged citizen

Transparency, linked to informed consumer expectations and choices, is an essential feature of standards requirements, since without it consumers cannot make informed choices about the content with which they engage. Reg Bailey's report, discussed above, referred to Ofcom's particular duties in developing media literacy, defined by Ofcom as 'the ability to use, understand and create communications.'[243] Under section 11 of the Communications Act 2003, Ofcom has a duty to promote media literacy and media literacy research informs three of Ofcom's strategic priorities set out in its Annual Plan 2011/2012: 'to provide appropriate assurance to audiences on standards; to help communications markets work for consumers; and to contribute and implement public policy as defined by Parliament'.[244]

However, Ofcom's January 2011 Media Literacy e-bulletin[245] noted that

> *In light of the recent economic review, Ofcom is currently reviewing its media literacy priorities for the new financial year. Reductions in our funding mean that some elements of Ofcom's media literacy work, such as funding initiatives, will inevitably have to be scaled back.*

In order to place such work on a secure financial footing, Eve Salomon saw a role for a literacy levy, funded by industry, as part of a quid pro quo for moves away from comprehensive statutory regulation. The Gambling Act,[246] she argued, may be instructive:

> *There's a statutory objective [under the Gambling Act] to protect children and the vulnerable. Gambling operators are expected to contribute to a fund to be used for research, education and treatment. If the industry doesn't cough up, there's a statutory backstop power to impose a levy.*[247]

In practice the gambling operators avoid an imposed levy and proactively fund a range of research, education, and treatment initiatives.[248] Such a model could equally be used to promote consumer media awareness, protection of children and the vulnerable, and training for providers. In Stephen Whittle's view (and as reflected in Nick Catliff's observations explored above) the latter is a significant area of concern:

> *One of the bigger challenges for BBC in particular, but broadcasters in general, is that because of the way the work force now is both recruited and retained, it is much more difficult to ensure an editorial culture which understands both ethical journalism and impartiality requirements, and the unique role of BBC ... With the way in which people aren't trained any more, or the way in which they are trained, it seems to me, largely by osmosis, it's going to be an increasing challenge, because there's a problem of culture and there's also a problem of loyalty. Do people understand the nature of what public service broadcasting is or should be? As opposed to simply being desperate to work in television. One of the unintended consequences of*

[243] http://stakeholders.ofcom.org.uk/market-data-research/media-literacy/about/whatis.
[244] http://www.ofcom.org.uk/files/2011/04/annplan1112.pdf.
[245] http://stakeholders.ofcom.org.uk/binaries/research/media-literacy/media-literacy-bulletin/mlb-issue-41.pdf.
[246] http://www.uk-gambling-act-2005.co.uk/s-N.
[247] Interview May 2011.
[248] http://www.gamblingcommission.gov.uk/gf-useful_links/problem_gambling.aspx.

producer choice and the independent quota system has been some of the more egregious scandals that we've seen.[249]

Such a levy could thus underpin consumer transparency and provider training, as well as promoting further development of technology, and awareness campaigns that serve the interests of children and young people as well as adults. As a minimum, Richard Sambrook observed:

> *You have to end up driving media literacy and education so that at least people can understand what it is they are consuming. It's like junk food – people can still go and buy [it] but at least they need to know what's in it ... you have the skills to recognise what's being pushed at you.[250]*

9.10. Aspirational coalition across media

Professor George Brock, Head of Journalism at City University and former Managing Editor and International Editor at *The Times,* took the notion of voluntary regulation a step further in envisaging a framework for news providers regardless of the platforms on which they publish: 'There will be a strong incentive for quality publications to come together, even if they do it voluntarily, around a core set of principles ... which they all hold in common.'[251]

Statutory regulation could be replaced, he argued, by 'aspirational coalition' with 'law at the corners', and could work across different news providers, who aspire to the same standards: '*The Times, Guardian, FT*, ITN, Bloomberg, Reuters will say "we subscribe to this set of principles" ... and an ombudsman will report whether they've kept to their own standards.'

Similarly, Martin Moore of the Media Standards Trust proposed a voluntary network across platforms for providers of news and other content. His starting point was a baseline of regulation determined by two factors:

> *One is the degree to which any media outlet benefits from some sort of indirect or direct subsidy so there is a quid pro quo. And equally, one has to begin to judge things by the size of audience and inevitably the greater audience brings with it greater responsibility ... [taking] into account the audience size relative to the community it is serving.*

Layered on top of this baseline of regulation he argued for self-regulation. Like Brock, he considered that a self-regulatory framework would have to reflect the standards to which its members voluntarily aspired, and could not seek to impose standards determined by others since: 'Why on earth would anybody want to be part of a self regulatory structure that wasn't aspirational? Because the alternative is [just] a constraint to prevent me from competing on what's now a level playing field on the net.' He explained:

> *What we would like to encourage are aspirational self-regulatory networks. You might get five or ten different publishers who all have very high standards in terms of what they feel is their obligation to their readers or audience and how they feel they have fulfilled those standards. And they get*

[249] Interview May 2011.
[250] Interview May 2011.
[251] Interview May 2011.

together and agree together what those high standards are and they make them very clear and transparent on their website or on their programmes. And it might be that there's also a revenue and income potential with that, because they can negotiate with search engines or others and say, it's worth you making [our adherence to these standards] clear to your readers, or actually bumping us up in the search results because we adhere to these standards unlike someone else who doesn't.' So people do it because they think it will increase trust in their users and it will give them a point of leverage with third parties and aggregators, search engines and others which will give them some revenue benefit.[252]

For Moore, 'metadata' is an essential part of moving towards these self-regulatory networks. He has previously observed:

Metadata is just a fancy word for information about information. A library catalogue is metadata because it categorizes the books and describes where you can find them. You find metadata on the side of every food packet, only we don't call it metadata, we call it ingredients. The equivalent metadata about a news article would capture information about where it was written, who wrote it, when it was first published, when it was updated. All pretty basic stuff, but critical to properly identifying it and helping its distribution.[253]

The Media Standards Trust has been developing ways of implementing metadata in order that:

Every news article has consistent information about who wrote it, who published it, when it was published etc. built into it. Every article also has an embedded link to the license associated with its reuse (so ignorance is no excuse). And, every article has a link to the principles to which it adheres. These principles should not only help to distinguish the article as journalism, but should make the principles that define journalism – that are right now opaque and little understood by the public – transparent. Moreover, all this information is made 'machine-readable' [so that] a machine (like a search engine) can understand it.[254]

In this way, Moore argued, the regulatory standards (whether statutory, voluntary, or a combination) to which a piece of content (text or audiovisual) adhered could be signalled to the consumer. This information could also be coordinated by Ofcom, or a media complaints portal, that could direct consumers to the relevant regulatory body and provide performance measurements. Moore's proposals envisage a role for an informed, enabled consumer, but also keep 'protection' to the baseline referred to above. Moore argued that public providers in receipt of any sort of direct or indirect public subsidy should be required to make it transparent that they benefit from such a subsidy, and therefore adhere to particular obligations and responsibilities. For all other media he did not see a role for a standards or 'kite' mark because such standards would be voluntarily aspired to, rather than externally enforced:

---

[252] Interview May 2011.

[253] http://martinjemoore.com/how-metadata-can-eliminate-the-need-for-pay-walls.

[254] http://martinjemoore.com/how-metadata-can-eliminate-the-need-for-pay-walls.

In the digital media world I always steer clear of the idea of a kite mark because the completely natural and unanswerable question is who upholds the standards? It's just so difficult in a world where anyone can publish, and inevitably there's going to be more and more blurring between professional and amateur content, and a mixture of the two. As we've seen with Twitter and elsewhere, the degree to which the platform operator takes responsibility versus the degree to which the person who has produced the content, is really quite hard.

The network of self-regulatory coalitions proposed by Moore, supported by metadata tagged to individual content, provides an exciting glimpse into a brave new world of empowered citizens and providers. Indeed tagged content could be separately aggregated, creating a regulated space for consumers.

However, such ideas are also a huge leap from current regulatory protections. Chapter 10 below argues for a managed transition, which opens the way to such possibilities in the future, while remaining sensitive to current consumer concerns and expectations, and responsive to emerging developments in consumer attitudes. It acknowledges the chain of responsibility – from platform operator to content aggregator to content producer – to which Martin Moore refers. It suggests that the link between editorial responsibility and media service providers made by the AVMS Directive (and currently applied by ATVOD to video on demand material) may provide useful lessons in determining and defining responsibility for regulatory compliance in the online environment, whether the provider's background has been founded in a broadcast, print, video on demand, or online medium.

10. Recommendations

This review has identified a blended media environment in which different sources of media content are subject to different regulatory requirements, and yet it is increasingly difficult to distinguish this content, identify the regulatory regime at play, or justify the range of different regulatory obligations applied. It is an environment in which consumer expectations are running out of kilter with the reality of regulation, and in which models of regulation derived from concerns about a monopoly of information and influence in the 1950s underpin a multi-channel, multi-platform world 60 years on. Structures for complaint-handling illustrate the bewildering array of separate regulatory codes and bodies with which consumers and providers must engage. Meanwhile, media content is increasingly converging on the same space, illustrated most significantly by the advent of internet-connected television.

Amidst such complexity, and at times duplication and contradiction of regulation, the consideration being given to the next Communications Act, and to such investigations as the Leveson Inquiry, provides a timely opportunity to consider afresh the key regulatory purposes across the media landscape and devise a new settlement for its regulation. Consumers, particularly younger consumers, are engaging with content in new ways, not as passive recipients but as active participants. New media encourage professional and amateur journalism to meet in debate on websites, in blogs, through Twitter, and in a myriad of ways to come. However, without a consistent, proportionate and transparent settlement for media regulation, receptive to new providers, the ability to discriminate between sources of content is wholly compromised. Consumer confidence and trust is put at risk, not just in content and its regulation but in the public space in which the democratic conversation is conducted and in which the right 'to receive' as well as to 'impart' information and ideas[255] is exercised.

The next Communications Act faces the difficulty and opportunity of distilling what we value about the journalism and the 'public space' in which it sits, and regulating it, consistently and proportionately, across platforms.

Significantly, the new settlement for media regulation has the potential to:

1. Acknowledge the value of public service content across platforms, recognise the high expectations placed on it and regulate it proportionately and consistently.
2. Recognise the value of a plurality of approaches to content regulation from public and commercial providers (whether from a broadcasting, print, video on demand, or wider online background): reflecting statutory requirements where applicable, while also incentivising commitments to voluntary standards that allow journalism, and related content, to flourish.

---

[255] European Convention on Human Rights can be found at: http://www.echr.coe.int/NR/rdonlyres/D5CC24A7-DC13-4318-B457-5C9014916D7A/0/ENG_CONV.pdf.

3. Reconcile the generational differences between consumers who approach content with old media or new media expectations.

4. Support new content providers, who have no current regulatory obligations, in differentiating their contributions to public debate.

5. Recognise that while reducing regulatory burdens in some areas and increasing regulatory expectations in others will present challenges, this will replace confusion and uncertainty (and a growing sense of powerlessness amongst consumers) with coherence and consistency across a dynamic media landscape.

6. Promote trust in the democratic conversation by offering consumers the opportunity to discriminate between the regulated and unregulated public space in order to make informed choices about the range of content provision, while providing appropriate protection for children.

Informed choice for consumers and incentivised choice for providers offer the keys to the regulatory dilemmas we face. The approach proposed here moves media regulation towards a world which *narrows statutory regulation* (setting out comprehensive 'premium standard' requirements for public service media across platforms, and 'baseline' requirements for television and video on demand agreed at a European level) but complements it with *independent regulation based on voluntary commitments by industry and recognition in statute* for private media, whether from a newspaper, broadcasting, video on demand, or online tradition. It proposes a framework in which *citizens exercise informed choice* over their engagement with regulated and unregulated content, supported by transparent messaging; which *protects children* and young people and in which *media providers make incentivised choices* over whether adherence to voluntary standards is commercially and ethically valuable, through association with a range of benefits and privileges. It recognises the traditions from which different providers have developed, and consumer expectations have formed, and *supports transition* towards a transparently signposted, plural, consistent *regulatory framework across media platforms*.

10.1. Enabling adults, protecting children

The framing of the current Communications Act, and therefore Ofcom's duties, within a general context of 'adequate protection' of both children and adults sets a tone that is out of joint with both the range of content available across platforms, and with the invitation provided by the technology actively to connect with it. Running through the current Communications Act is a blurring between protections that are necessary, most importantly recognising the vulnerability of children, and protections that unhelpfully cast adults as passive consumers on whom content is imposed.

Instead, the informed choices of adult consumers should be positively promoted. Not as an 'add-on', as is currently the case in relation to media literacy's place in the current Act, but rather placing consumer confidence and understanding right at the heart of the new Act. And such choices could be actively supported through transparency of regulatory requirements and clarity of labelling (discussed further below). In this way, navigating content (regulated and unregulated) across platforms would be more than a demonstration of 'media literacy', it would play a central role in democratic engagement across the public space provided by the media.

Under the proposals here, protection of children and young people would be set out in the Act as a distinct concern, and linked to the range of other means by which children in our society are protected. In this way the current elision between 'harm and offence' would be struck through. Harm (whether of children or vulnerable adults) requires very different approaches to offence (where labelling, access controls, and in the case of linear content, scheduling, offer a range of tools). Similarly, fairness and privacy responsibilities would not be framed in the language of protection, rather the new Communications Act would require a recognition of the, at times, competing demands of freedom of expression on the one hand, and fair dealing and the right to privacy on the other.

The task of a new communications settlement will also be to manage transition: enabling consumers, and indeed providers and regulators, to play catch-up with technological advances and content convergence.

As George Brock put it:

> *You have to remember when you get these phases of deep change driven by new, enabling technology, what you get is successive waves of change. It's not one change, where you can see a phase of change and then it stops. It's rolling waves of change. It comes in like the sea so you need something that is approximately best ... to deal with that.*[256]

The proposed approach invites the Communications Act to manage transition by establishing a statutory framework that is to designed to develop flexibly over time, thereby retaining the confidence of both consumers and providers.

Initially, the new Act would establish a framework that would retain the familiar notions of broadcasting, newspaper, video on demand, and online content, but would introduce a tiered framework for media regulation signalled by readily identifiable standards marks online, in print, and on EPGs. Consumers would be supported in distinguishing regulated from unregulated content and making choices accordingly. A summary of the proposed initial framework is set out in Figure 10.1 below and discussed in the next sections.

The proposal would be for the new Communications Act to be framed in such a way that, over time, the three tiers of regulation, as indicated above, would develop beyond associations with 'broadcasting', 'newspapers', and 'video on demand' material. Instead, the tiers would apply to content across media platforms. I have argued that the application of different regulatory standards to different media delivery platforms was historically logical but increasingly lacks coherence. The approach proposed is to develop the initial framework set out above for content and providers, across platforms, differentiated by their *values* not their modes of *distribution*. The result is transition to a tiered regulatory framework under which media content, whether it has originated in broadcasting, print, video on demand, or online, is regulated coherently and consistently.

10.2. Tier 1: distinct cross-platform public service provision

Transition to cross-platform Tier 1 regulation: Under these proposals the new Communications Act would set out comprehensive 'premium standard' requirements of public service content (across broadcasting, video on demand and online platforms). Initially Tier 1 regulation would be associated with all broadcasters, however, the Act would provide for any commercial broadcaster, without public service obligations, to elect regulation under Tiers 2 or 3 as these develop over time. Equally, and by contrast to current broadcasting regulation, it would be receptive to providers who might wish to elect future Tier 1 regulation, as a mark of standards, quality, and impartiality, whether from a print, video on demand, or wider online background.

[256] Interview May 2011.

Standards Mark	Delivery/provider	Requirements	Benefits	Regulation
Tier 1	Broadcasting	Comprehensive requirements including protection of minors and vulnerable adults, offence, accuracy, impartiality, incitement, fairness, privacy and commercial communications. Equivalent to the current Ofcom Code rules (and therefore implementing the AVMS Directive) but framed in relation to enabling adults, protecting children.	• Requirements shift from current 'public protection' objectives to 'enabling adults, protecting children'. • Consumers introduced to the tiered framework and its standards marks, and supported in making informed choices about regulated and unregulated content. • Act would set standards for public service content across platforms and permit non public service broadcasters to migrate to Tier 2 or Tier 3 models of regulation as these develop over time, or to elect to remain within Tier 1. • Equally it would be receptive to non-broadcast providers adopting Tier 1 regulation over time.	**Statutory standards regulation** Requirements framed in legislation; administered and enforced by a regulator with statutory powers.
Tier 2	Newspapers	Requirements could include privacy, fairness, separation of fact and opinion; accuracy in news, right of reply, prohibition on incitement, protection of minors, standards on ethical practices.	• Provision of print/online/electronic newspaper offerings that are subject to consistent, ethical standards readily understood by consumers. • Incentivised through, for example, Tier 2 membership being taken into account by the courts in privacy proceedings; accreditation in relation to court and other reporting; favourable advertising and search engine associations; potential charitable and taxation concessions; differentiation from Tier 3 and unregulated content. • Over time titles could elect Tier 1 or 3 models of regulation or remain within Tier 2.	**Independent standards regulation** Requirements framed by industry; administered and enforced by a regulator recognised in statute, but whose powers derive from the voluntary acceptance of its jurisdiction by Tier 2 members.
Tier 3	Video on demand (VOD)	A slim set of statutory requirements which could include right of reply, prohibition on incitement, some commercial restrictions, protection of minors (implementing European AVMS Directive requirements).	• Provision of content to which a consistent baseline of standards applies (across VOD services). Implements the AVMS requirements. • Act would support VOD providers in electing Tier 1 or 2 models of regulation or remaining in Tier 3.	**Statutory standards regulation** Requirements framed in legislation; administered and enforced by a regulator with statutory powers.
Unregulated content	Providers not electing, or caught by, the requirements of Tiers 1 to 3	Criminal and civil law applies (and any ad hoc arrangements outside them to make informed choices about engagement with unregulated content.	• Any providers not carrying Tier 1, 2 or 3 standards marks would be readily distinguishable by consumers, enabling them to make informed choices about engagement with unregulated content.	Bodies such as the IWF continue to work to minimise the availability of criminal content.

Figure 10.1: Summary of Proposal for an Initial Tiered Standards Framework under a New Communications Act

Under this approach a new communications settlement would provide a clear understanding of the value, and expectation, of 'public' content providers. Obligations linked to access to spectrum, undermined by digital switchover and challenged by alternative online platforms, have run their course. Under the approach proposed here, regulatory requirements would differentiate between those services in which there is a public interest, for example though public ownership, funding and/or subject to public service obligations (linked for example to public service multiplex access discussed in Chapter 1), and those that represent purely private interests and have no public service obligations. This would herald a new compact which would narrow the scope of comprehensive statutory regulation, and its associated consumer expectations, to public providers.

The BBC (including the World Service following changes to its funding), Channel 4, and S4C would all fall into this category, as would ITV and Channel 5 for as long as they choose to retain public service obligations.[257] Under the approach proposed here, commercial public service providers would be incentivised to continue to maintain their commitment to public service provision and would continue to benefit from EPG prominence and a place on the public service multiplexes which, as discussed in Chapter 1, provide greatest access to audiences. Standards requirements would be part of the expectations placed on them, but would also provide a transparent demonstration of excellence and authority for domestic and, potentially, international audiences, associating them with media organisations under public ownership and differentiating their offerings from the rest of the industry discussed below.

In relation to all 'public' providers, the new media settlement envisaged here would recognise that online is not a bolt-on to traditional content, but is integral to public service provision. The regulation of 'public' providers would apply across the 'public space' and therefore across platforms including radio, television, video on demand, and other online output from the same brand, for example, ITV, ITV Player, itv.com. All such output would be associated with a standards mark to denote the level of regulatory requirements. Such a standards mark would be linked to service providers, and also used to label individual content, for example, BBC content on YouTube, or publicly funded programmes provided by any content aggregators. Increasingly sophisticated 'metadata' tagging, discussed in Chapter 9 above, would assist in identifying material regulated under this standards mark and aggregating it into a 'regulated online space' for consumers.

While public content would entertain and amuse, what would underpin its contribution to society would be its ability, and duty, across platforms, to inform, challenge, inspire, and connect.[258] Public providers would be expected to play a role in supporting consumers to navigate online content and to counter concerns that fragmented new media, as explored in Chapter 6 above, serve to reinforce prejudices and narrow horizons. This ability to direct users out to other viewpoints builds on the democratic promotion of a diversity of viewpoints (hitherto linked to impartiality requirements) and the traditional role of public service providers in this respect.

In distinguishing public content, and its regulation, the Act could set out a comprehensive set of rules for Tier 1 regulation that might not be dissimilar to the range

---

[257] Despite commercial pressures on public services broadcasters, both ITV and Channel 5 have indicated the value in retaining a PSB licence, e.g. channel prominence on EPG's, guaranteed access to public service multiplexes and association with the BBC and Channel 4 (June 2011 Westminster Media Forum seminar, 'Public Service Content – Priorities for the Communications Bill': http://www.westminsterforumprojects.co.uk/forums/showpublications.php?pid=315).

[258] As set out in the Digital Economy Act which recognises Channel 4's cross-platform duties, e.g. to: 'support and stimulate well-informed debate on a wide range of issues, including by providing access to information and views from around the world and by challenging established views, promote alternative views and new perspectives', whether on 'television programme services ... on-demand programme services or other services by means of the internet': http://www.legislation.gov.uk/ukpga/2010/24/section/22.

of provisions of the current Ofcom Broadcasting Code, but whose first principles would focus on positive engagement with media instead of protection from it, as discussed above, and would incorporate the basic requirements of the AVMS Directive. Impartiality requirements could be developed to provide cross-platform access to balanced coverage and a range of viewpoints on issues of particular significance. The comprehensive standards would be set out in statute and both administered and enforced by a regulator with statutory powers.

There are complex related matters that would require attention. In particular, any regulatory duplications with the BBC Trust would need to be removed, any additional requirements voluntarily adhered to by the BBC would have to be clear to consumers, and particular arrangements made for the regulation of commercial providers with public service commitments (discussed above), and for local television.

In addition, as set out for the second and third tiers below, a key feature of the proposed approach is that it would be open to other providers to seek regulation under the standards requirements for public services. A news agency, a journalist, a newspaper, or a commercial broadcaster whose selling point is their impartiality, could elect regulation under this top tier of standards, and accept the sanctions, including fines, that could be imposed in the event of code breaches. In exchange for adhering to the demanding nature of its requirements, they would benefit from association with the public service providers, the range of privileges in relation to accreditation and other incentives set out in relation to Tier 2 regulation below, privileged positioning on EPGs where appropriate, and differentiation of their content from those of providers in other tiers, leading to enhanced advertising associations as well as public recognition.

10.3. Tier 2: ethical private media

Transition to cross-platform Tier 2 regulation: Under these proposals a new Communications Act would recognise an independent regulator for voluntary standards. Initially Tier 2 would establish robust, independent regulation for the press, underpinned by the principles detailed in Chapter 4 (independence, both of industry and the state; statutory recognition in order to secure both its authority and independence; voluntary membership incentivised through a range of benefits and privileges; transparent messaging for consumers in print and online; and a range of sanctions and investigatory procedures). Over time press members could seek Tier 1 regulation if that more closely fitted their values and aspirations, or they could seek the more limited regulation under Tier 3 and sacrifice the benefits and privileges conferred by a commitment to Tier 2 standards. Similarly, the proposal would be that this tier of regulation would be receptive over time to broadcasters, video on demand providers, or currently unregulated online providers who might naturally seek a place within it.

As discussed earlier, the current UK models raise a number of problems in relation to the private media sector: comprehensive statutory regulation is a better fit with the public duties associated with public services than to a one-size-fits-all approach to broadcasting; self-regulation has suffered blow after blow under the PCC model; and co-regulation by ATVOD provides only the most basic of regulation in relation to editorial content. On the other hand, a statutory basis for regulation can strengthen it; voluntary regulation that casts standards as a selling point incentivises buy-in and real commitment from its members, and can be highly responsive to change; and the ATVOD model provides a working basis for cross-media definitions and requirements.

The regulation proposed under Tier 2 would be based on voluntary, incentivised, transparent, ethical media standards. It would invite consumers to make informed choices about the content with which they engage and providers to consider the advantages of public recognition under the following key principles (also explored in Chapter 4 in relation to press regulation):

- Independence: the proposed model would provide regulation that is independent, both of industry and the state, in its administration and enforcement of regulatory requirements. It would be funded, and its rules established, by industry, but the independence of its decision-making and robustness of its sanctions would be guaranteed, for example, through the chairman and the composition of its board members and by procedures for dealing with complaints and investigations.
- Statutory recognition: while the proposed model of regulation would be entirely independent of government and the state, it would be provided with recognition in statute. This would afford a secure foundation for its authority and independence. It would not, however, confer statutory powers since the basis for its authority would be voluntary membership. Providers, from newspapers to bloggers to, eventually, broadcasters, would not be required to accept its jurisdiction. Instead they would, as discussed below, be highly incentivised in doing so.
- Transparency: this would be a core requirement enabling the consumer to discriminate between providers who have made a commitment to regulatory requirements and those who have rejected such a commitment. Transparency would be achieved through an associated standards mark clearly flagged in print and online.
- Incentivised voluntary participation: private content providers in Tier 2 would have the choice of electing standards as a selling point and enjoying associated benefits. Benefits and privileges attached to such membership would require detailed consideration but could include: recognition by the courts in relation to demonstrating responsible journalism in privacy and libel cases; the ability to attract favourable advertising associations; accreditation in relation to court reporting and other privileged access to information; potential taxation and charitable incentives; and association with other regulated media, thereby differentiating their offerings from unregulated content.
- Credible investigations and sanctions: in return for the benefits of membership, Tier 2 providers would be required to agree and accept a range of sanctions and investigatory procedures at the disposal of the new regulatory body, including suspension and expulsion from its membership and associated benefits.

Initially, as explored in Chapter 4, this approach would be proposed as a model of independent, statutorily recognised press regulation. However, over time, the proposal would be to extend it to the regulation of private (commercial, non-public service) media hitherto regulated according to broadcasting or video on demand regulation. It would also be receptive to currently unregulated providers wishing to be affiliated with it as discussed below. Similarly new and existing newspaper members could elect future regulation under Tiers 1 or 3 if that more closely mirrored their values and commercial choices.

The approach here is to de-link non-'public' broadcasting from the current system of licences which, as we have seen, is challenged both by digital switchover and alternative online opportunities. Instead, a model of the notification approach, currently required of video on demand services under ATVOD as discussed in Chapter 5, could be extended to linear television and radio services. The criteria for notification might include provision of programmes, editorial responsibility, scheduling/cataloguing, provision to the public via an electronic communications network – all notions used to define linear and on demand audiovisual media services under the AVMS Directive (discussed in Chapters 3 and 5) but also applicable to radio content. The Directive would thus provide useful criteria against which to measure content, forming part of the regulated audio/audiovisual 'public space' without relying on traditional notions of broadcasting. The proposal would be to apply consistency to scheduled and video on demand material, and the regulation of video on demand material would no longer be parasitic (as discussed in Chapter 5) on a scheduled, linear Broadcasting Code, as is the case at present.

The standards to which Tier 2 members would make a commitment would be framed by the industry itself, reflecting its mutual interests with its consumers. These could include rules in relation to privacy, separation of fact and opinion, accuracy in news, a right of reply and ethical conduct (including requirements not dissimilar to the current PCC Code), and nuanced to take account of the differing contexts of printed, scheduled, and video on demand services and wider entertainment and other providers. For example, a watershed for scheduled content could be applied, and labelling and access controls provided. Transparency over complaints, adjudications, and sanctions (for example, requirements to publish adjudications and membership suspension) would be required. The aim would be for standards to be a selling point: a commercial advantage in attracting advertising and, potentially, search engine associations, and sensitive to consumer demand.

While adherence to Tier 2 regulation would be incentivised for the press, and transparently understood by consumers, press regulation under any of the tiers would be entirely a matter of choice. However, for non-public service broadcast and video on demand providers, this framework acknowledges that statutory requirements placed on them (for example, under the European AVMS Directive discussed above), would require adherence. This model proposes that any breaches of those baseline requirements would be referred to the Tier 3 regulator that would have statutory powers of enforcement.

10.4. Tier 3: baseline private media

Transition to cross-platform Tier 3 regulation: Under these proposals the new Communications Act would set out baseline requirements, consistent with the demands of European agreements placed on broadcast and video on demand services. These requirements (for as long as they remain 'delivery-specific') would be set out in statute and administered and enforced by a regulator with statutory powers. Broadcasters or video on demand providers within Tier 2 found to have breached these statutory requirements would be referred to the Tier 3 regulator. Over time Tier 3 video on demand providers seeking enhanced regulation (and benefits) could opt in to a higher tier; broadcasting or print providers wishing to level down could join Tier 3; and currently unregulated providers could opt in to it (discussed further below).

Inevitably, the voluntary model of independent regulation proposed for Tier 2 raises the possibility that some players will not see an advantage in becoming, or remaining, a member. For those deciding not to adhere to its voluntary commitment to standards, baseline requirements would apply to broadcasters and video on demand providers (including newspaper providers) as set out in the AVMS Directive. The third tier standards mark would denote the basic standards required of these providers. It would readily identify, for consumers, those providers of broadcast and video on demand services that have not taken on additional Tier 2 commitments, but also differentiate them from unregulated content.

10.5. A consumer confidence levy

The proposed approach demands a clear understanding by consumers of each of the three tiers of 'public', 'ethical private', and 'baseline' regulation; transparency is at the core of such an understanding. Consumer research demonstrates that expectations of the BBC are already clearly different to those of other providers and an appreciation of the 'public' content requirements should be relatively straightforward. However, an understanding of the regulatory framework for video on demand material is more limited, and the wider proposed approach to 'private' voluntary regulation across broadcast, print, video on demand, and other online services would be wholly new. A clear understanding of the new regulatory framework on the part of consumers and providers would not be achieved by bolted on 'media literacy', nor by the vagaries of funding in relation to its promotion, discussed in Chapter 9.

Instead, consumer understanding, and related provider compliance training, could be underpinned by a 'consumer confidence levy' akin to the gambling levy discussed above. This would support research, education, and training initiatives and underpin the standards marks for the three tiers of regulation which would be required to be clearly signalled. Such transparency would remove reliance on, and assumptions around, well-known brands as an indication of standards, and therefore of quality. These can, as we have seen, be both misleading and unhelpful in relation to new and less established providers. The standards marks could be clearly signposted online and on the EPG. Consumers could be enabled to place access controls over, or simply block, content within the different tiers (just as adult services can be removed from the Sky and Virgin Media EPGs). The standards marks would sit alongside labelling and information for individual content that could include an age certification system similar to that provided by BBFC film certification.

The public would be supported in understanding the regulatory requirements of, and linked complaints mechanisms in relation to, each standards tier. Significantly, they would also be provided with a secure basis for expectations in relation to content, and supported in understanding the limitations of regulation in order confidently to recognise and navigate unregulated media content. Meanwhile training for providers would provide a clear understanding of the requirements expected of them in order to embed recognition of their rights and responsibilities.

10.6. An inclusive regulatory framework open to emerging electronic media providers

As discussed in relation to each of the tiers of regulation above, the regulatory framework under this proposed approach would be open to media providers not caught by compulsory requirements to elect to sign up to any of the three tiers of regulation, or elect to join a tier offering enhanced regulation if that is considered advantageous. For example, an unregulated online provider could elect to sign up to the third tier standards mark, to signal its regard for the baseline requirements.

Size would not, under this model, determine regulatory duties; however, a large, mainstream, private news provider might seek to differentiate and enhance its offering by choosing to adhere to the comprehensive 'public' code, including, for example, requirements around impartiality. Broadsheets and tabloids could, eventually, opt for regulation under different tiers depending on which most closely reflected their values and content. An online journalist could use adherence to the voluntary regulation of Tier 2 as a means of demonstrating accreditation. Providers would be able to differentiate their material by reference to the values and standards to which they subscribe.

Standards Mark	Delivery/provider	Requirements	Benefits	Regulation
Tier 1 Premium 'public' content	**Compulsory** requirements for public service (publicly or privately owned) TV, radio, VOD and related online/electronic content.	Comprehensive statutory requirements including protection of minors and vulnerable adults, offence, accuracy, impartiality, incitement, fairness, privacy and commercial communications. Equivalent to the requirements of the current Ofcom Code (and therefore implementing the AVMS Directive), enabling adults, protecting children.	• Provision of content (across platforms) that is subject to consistent, comprehensive decision-making as well as wider entertainment and information.	**Statutory 'premium standard' regulation** Comprehensive standards required of public service providers across platforms (and elected by other providers); framed in legislation; administered and enforced by a regulator with statutory powers.
	Opt-in for non-public service commercial television and radio; newspapers; VOD; and other online/electronic content.		• Opt-in providers benefit from favourable association with public service content; differentiation from Tier 2 and 3 content; EPG prominence and PSB multiplex access for broadcasters; demonstration of values and excellence for others including the quality press.	
Tier 2 Ethical 'private' content	**Opt-in** for non-public service commercial TV* and radio*; VOD providers*; newspapers* and other online/ electronic content	Requirements could include privacy, fairness, separation of fact and opinion; accuracy in news, right of reply, prohibition on incitement, some commercial restrictions, protection of minors, standards on ethical practices. (Includes some compulsory requirements of compulsory for broadcast and/or VOD services as set out in Tier 3).	• Provision of content (across scheduled and VOD services; online and print newspaper offerings; and new media providers) that is subject to consistent, ethical standards readily understood by consumers. • Incentivised through, for example, Tier 2 membership being taken into account by the courts in privacy proceedings; accreditation in relation to the voluntary acceptance of its jurisdiction by Tier 2 members.	**Independent 'ethical standard' regulation** Standards framed by industry; administered and enforced by a regulator recognised in statute but whose powers derive from the Tier 3 regulator.
	(*denotes also subject to the compulsory requirements of Tier 3).		• Differentiation from Tier 3 and unregulated content; and, for broadcasters, favourable advertising and search engine associations; potential charitable and taxation concessions; differentiation from Tier 3 and associated EPG positioning.	Broadcasters and VOD providers in breach of their Tier 3 basic requirements would be referred to the Tier 3 regulator.
Tier 3 Baseline 'private' content	**Compulsory** requirements for privately owned TV, radio and VOD services.	A slim set of statutory requirements which could include right of reply, prohibition on incitement, some commercial restrictions, protection of minors (implementing European requirements and providing a baseline for radio).	• Provision of content to which a consistent baseline of standards applies (across scheduled and VOD services). Implements the European AVMS requirements.	**Statutory 'baseline' regulation** Standards consistent with European requirements; required of some providers, elected by others; administered and enforced by a regulator with statutory powers.
	Opt in for currently unregulated providers.		• Differentiates 'opt in' content, including newspaper offerings, from unregulated content.	
Unregulated content	Providers not electing, or caught by, Tiers 1 to 3	Criminal and civil law applies (and any ad hoc arrangements outside of the tiered framework).	• Unregulated content readily distinguishable from regulated content carrying the Tiers 1 to 3 standards marks, enabling consumer and provider choices.	Bodies such as the IWF continue to work to minimise criminal content availability.

Figure 10.2.: Summary of Proposal for an Eventual Cross-Platform Values-Based Standards Framework under a New Communications Act

The standards marks would provide not just mainstream providers but, significantly, new brands with transparent messaging for the public. Similarly, the relevant standards mark would be clearly flagged on websites, easily identifying providers subscribing to each tier, and attached to individual content provided via online content aggregators. The proposed framework is not limited to audiovisual material, but would be offered to any electronic media provider as the media landscape develops.

Figure 10.2 summarises the proposal for the eventual cross-platform, values-based framework discussed in this chapter. The approach proposed invites commercial providers to consider the advantages of independent regulation, of association with other similarly regulated content producers and thereby attracting advertising associations. It invites bloggers and other new media participants to benefit from accreditation through regulatory affiliation; broadcasters to benefit from associated EPG ranking; consumers to engage with a framework that is responsive to complaints, providing a place for informal resolution as well as more formal sanctions for breaches of the codes associated with each tier; citizens to be provided with an informed basis on which to base media expectations and engagement; regulators to resolve current areas of confusion and inconsistency; and forthcoming legislation to promote a coherent and transparent approach to media regulation.

10.7. In conclusion

This work has sought to demonstrate the opportunity provided by the next Communications Act, combined with the range of inquiries and consultations that have marked 2011, to frame a new settlement for the media and for the consumer.

For broadcasting it could remove the anachronistic basis of current legislation that unhelpfully pits the public, cast in a passive role requiring protection, against broadcasters, requiring restraint. Instead, it would protect children while acknowledging the ways in which new media have opened up opportunities for wide-ranging, active participation from all quarters. It would seek to enable consumers and providers to engage with the media in ways that are democratically and commercially valuable, informed, and incentivised, within the context of tiered requirements. For video on demand provision it would provide a framework that enables a consistent approach to standards across the public space. For print journalism it envisages a robust and incentivised regulatory framework that allows regulated newspaper offerings to be differentiated from unregulated, regardless of the means by which they are distributed, and applies regulation that is independent of both the industry and the state. For new media players it offers standards as a mark of accreditation and ethical values elected on a voluntary basis.

Overall, the proposed approach would see, not a 'rolling out' of current broadcasting regulation to other media, nor a 'rolling back' of current comprehensive requirements, but instead would offer a redistribution of regulatory standards across the public space. Some comprehensively regulated broadcast content would be released from current obligations, other currently minimally (or un-)regulated content would be incentivised to 'level up'. The print media would be free to choose where to position itself while being incentivised to adhere to robustly enforced standards, as well as enabled over time to associate itself with regulation best suited to its values and aspirations. In this way consumers and providers alike would benefit from a transparent framework of standards for journalism and other content, which would underpin the flourishing, creative communications sector envisaged in the opening debates on the next Communications Act.[259]

---

[259] http://www.culture.gov.uk/images/publications/commsreview-open-letter_160511.pdf.

Together, media providers, regulators, consumers, the courts, and parliament have the opportunity to shape a democratic agenda that recognises the contribution made by journalism (and wider media content), values the public space it inhabits, and renews the regulation that sustains it.

Annex 1. Interviewees, May 2011

STEPHEN ABELL: Director, Press Complaints Commission

PAUL BRADSHAW: Publisher, the Online Journalism Blog; Founder, Help me Investigate (crowdsourcing website); Visiting Professor, City University

GEORGE BROCK: Professor and Head of Journalism, City University; Former Managing Editor, *The Times*

NICK CATLIFF: Managing Director, Lion Television

LIS HOWELL: Director of Broadcasting, City University; Former Director of Programmes, GMTV

PETE JOHNSON: Chief Executive Officer, ATVOD; Former Head of Policy, British Board of Film Classification

MARTIN MOORE: Director, Media Standards Trust

MATT PAYTON: Director of External Affairs, RadioCentre

STEWART PURVIS: Professor of Television Journalism, City University; Former Chief Executive, ITN; Former Partner for Content and Standards, Ofcom

EVE SALOMON: Chair, Internet Watch Foundation; Former Director of Legal Services, Radio Authority; Interim Secretary, Ofcom; and Commissioner, Press Complaints Commission; author, UNESCO Guidelines for Broadcasting Regulation

RICHARD SAMBROOK: Visiting Fellow, Reuters Institute for the Study of Journalism; Former Director, BBC Global News division

STEPHEN WHITTLE: Chair, Broadcasting Equality and Training Regulator; Former Controller, BBC Editorial Policy; Former Director, Broadcasting Standards Commission; Former Visiting Fellow, Reuters Institute for the Study of Journalism

Annex 2. Making Complaints about BBC and Other Media Services

Tables included in the House of Lords Select Committee on Communications Report, *The Governance and Regulation of the BBC*, June 2011.[260]

How to Complain about a BBC Service

Which service are you complaining about?	What are you complaining about?	Where to complain
BBC television or radio programmes on a BBC branded channel or radio station in the UK	Standards in programmes include fairness and privacy	BBC and/or Ofcom
	Accuracy and impartiality and commercial references	BBC
BBC television or radio programmes on a commercial broadcasting service licensed by Ofcom	Complaints about standards in programmes, commercial references, fairness and privacy, accuracy in news and impartiality in news and certain other subjects (e.g. public policy)	Ofcom
BBC iplayer	Complaints about incitement to racial hatred, material that might seriously impair under-18s and inappropriate commercial references	BBC or Ofcom
BBC content on a non-BBC player or VOD site (e.g. BT vision)	Complaints about incitement to racial hatred, material that might seriously impair under-18s and inappropriate commercial references	BBC first then ATVOD
BBC website (including BBC Worldwide website overseas)	All complaints about content	BBC
BBC radio programmes listened to online via RadioPlayer	All complaints about content	BBC
BBC World Service radio programmes	All complaints about content	BBC
All BBC magazines	All complaints about content	BBC and/or the PCC
BBC teenage magazines	All complaints about content	BBC and/or the PCC and/or TMAP
Advertising around BBC programmes shown on BBC Worldwide owned/part owned UK commercial channels	Complaints about content	ASA
	Complaints about timing	Ofcom
Political advertisements and some forms of long-form advertising (i.e. teleshopping) concerning adult, psychic and gambling services on BBC Worldwide channels in the UK	Complaints about content	Ofcom
Sponsorship on BBC programmes shown on BBC Worldwide owned/part-owned commercial channels in the UK	All complaints	Ofcom
TV licensing	Complaints about the administration of the licence fee collection service (not programming or reception quality complaints)	TV Licensing, with option to appeal to the BBC
Complaints about matters other than those covered by guidelines or codes	A variety of different issues, for example killing off a cast member in a TV or radio programme, ticketing policy, scheduling matters etc.)	BBC
Fair trading	All fair trading complaints	BBC
The Digital Switchover Help Scheme	The operation of the Help Scheme (complaints about policy are passed on to DCMS)	Switchover Help Scheme, with option to appeal to the BBC

[260] http://www.publications.parliament.uk/pa/ld201012/ldselect/ldcomuni/166/16606.htm (source: BBC, Ofcom, and ATVOD).

How to Complain about (Non-BBC) Media Services

Which service are you complaining about?	What are you complaining about?	Where to complain
Television programmes on all commercial broadcasting channels	Complaints about standards in programmes, commercial references, fairness and privacy, accuracy in news and impartiality in news and certain other subjects (e.g. public policy)	Broadcaster and/or Ofcom
Radio programmes on all commercial and community radio stations	Complaints about standards in programmes, commercial communications fairness and privacy, accuracy in news and impartiality in news and certain other subjects (e.g. public policy)	Broadcaster and/or Ofcom
Commercial radio programmes listened to online via RadioPlayer	Complaints about standards in programmes, commercial communications, fairness and privacy, accuracy in news and impartiality in news and certain other subjects (e.g. public policy)	Broadcaster
Television and radio programmes on commercial channels and on community radio stations	Complaints about premium rate services	Phonepay Plus
On-demand services providing 'TV-like' programmes (e.g. 4OD, ITV Player)	Complaints about material likely to encourage or incite the commission of crime or lead to disorder	ATVOD
	Complaints about incitement to hatred based on race, sex, religion or nationality; material that might seriously impair under-18s; and breaches of sponsorship or product placement rules	Service-provider first then ATVOD
	All other complaints	Service provider
Newspapers or magazines	All complaints about content	Publisher and/or PCC
Teenage magazines	All complaints about content	Publisher and/or PCC and/or TMAP
Advertisements across all media including television, radio, print and online	All complaints about content	ASA
Political advertisements on television or radio and some forms of long-form advertising (i.e. teleshopping) concerning adult, psychic and gambling services	All complaints about content	Ofcom
	Complaints about timing	Ofcom
All television and radio advertisements		
Websites	All complaints about content	Website provider
Audiovisual content on newspaper websites	All complaints about content	PCC (ATVOD has said that TV-like services on newspaper websites fall within its jurisdiction)
Reporter and newspaper tweets on newspaper websites	All complaints about content	Expected to brought under the regulation of the PCC later this year
Complaints about matters other than those covered by guidelines or codes	A variety of different issues, for example killing off a cast member in a TV or radio programme, ticketing policy, scheduling matters etc.)	BBC

Select Bibliography

Bailey, R., *Letting Children be Children* (TSO, 2011)

Bridcut, J., *From Seesaw to Wagon Wheel: Safeguarding Impartiality in the 21st Century* (BBC Trust, 2007)

Calcutt, D., *Review of Press Self-Regulation*, (HMSO, 1993)

Culture, Media and Sport Committee, *Press Standards, Privacy and Libel* (TSO, 2010)

Currah, A., *What's Happening to Our News* (RISJ, 2008)

Currie, D., 'The Principles and Objectives of a Converged Communications Regulator' (4th ECTA Regulatory Conference, 2003)

Essential Research, *The Regulation of Video-On-Demand* (Ofcom, 2009)

Foster, R., and T. Broughton, *Creative UK: The Audiovisual Sector and Economic Success* (Communications Chambers, 2011)

Gardam, T., and D. A. L. Levy (eds), *The Price of Plurality, Choice, Diversity and Broadcasting Institutions in the Digital Age* (RISJ, 2008)

Hargreaves, I., and J. Thomas, *New News, Old News* (ITC/BSC, 2002)

Information Commissioner's Office, *What Price Privacy? The Unlawful Trade in Confidential Personal Information* (ICO, 2006)

Murdoch, J., *The Absence of Trust* (MGEITF, 2009)

Ofcom and GfK, *The Consumer's Digital Day* (Ofcom, 2010)

Purvis, S., *Calling Time on Analogue Regulation: An Agenda for the Next Communications Act* (RTS, 2010)

Salomon, E., *Guidelines for Broadcasting Regulation* (CBA/UNESCO 2008)

Select Committee on Communications, *Inquiry into the Governance and Regulation of the BBC* (TSO, 2011)

Schmidt, E., *Television and the Internet: Shared Opportunity* (MGEITF, 2011)

Acknowledgements

I would like to thank those interviewed for this project for giving up their time, and contributing their reflections and expertise. The range of their perspectives was invaluable in shaping this report.

I would also like to thank David Levy of the Reuters Institute and Stewart Purvis of City University for their insightful comments and suggestions on drafting, and for their invaluable support and ideas throughout the project.

I am grateful to Jane Robson for her expert copy-editing, and to Alex Reid for ensuring that this publication was turned around speedily and smoothly. All mistakes are, of course, my own.

Other than the interviews, the research for this paper draws entirely on published material in the public domain. It represents my views as author rather than a statement of a collective view of either the Reuters Institute or City University, or any other body.

The future of media regulation will be a fascinating period of development. I hope that the ideas explored in this report will contribute to public debate and stimulate evolving thoughts and responses.